What people are saying about ...

Becoming NEW

"This devotional is like no other: it combines the mind and the heart, the best of doctrine applied to real life. I'm glad that Dan Jacobsen accepted the task of compiling this book left unfinished by his grandfather, Dr. Warren Wiersbe. As my predecessor, Pastor Wiersbe often blessed me with his books, and I welcome this one that is a heart-warming distillation of his wisdom and knowledge."

Dr. Erwin W. Lutzer, pastor emeritus,
The Moody Church

"When I first heard about *Becoming New*, one word came to mind: *treasure*. Warren Wiersbe mines God's Word and helps us see on each page that the work God wants to do in us is not behavior modification but full transformation. May this new book aid in that work in your heart and life."

Chris Fabry, author and host of *Chris Fabry Live*

"Dan Jacobson carefully curated the writings of his grandfather, Warren Wiersbe, to offer a devotional resource that guides the reader on a journey through the Old and New Testaments. This book will delight readers who are new to the understanding of Scripture yet also draw in those who have followed our Lord for some time. Wiersbe writes profoundly, with rich theological depth. My soul was nourished and strengthened while also being stirred to wonder and worship. It was a great joy to be taught again from this beloved pastor and teacher. This is sure to be a devotional that will be returned to again and again."

Dr. Pamela MacRae, professor at Moody Bible Institute

"One of the first books I read as a new Christian was a little commentary by Warren Wiersbe on the book of Philippians. I was sixteen years old—and didn't know my head from a hole in the ground. I'm forty-two today—and still as confused. But to come full-circle to read one of the first people who taught me to walk is an absolute gift. This devotional is a fitting tribute to a man who taught me to love Jesus and showed me the grace of God."

A. J. Swoboda, PhD, professor of Bible/theology at
Bushnell University, author of *The Gift of Thorns*

"When Dan told me he was embarking on this project, I couldn't think of a bigger challenge for him but also a greater reward for the kingdom as he and his grandfather influence and inspire us to deeper levels of intimacy with Jesus and bolder steps of faith. Just as I was challenged by Wiersbe years ago to grow and mature in Christ, I know that you will be encouraged to do the same. Whether you're investigating the faith, just getting started, or have been walking with God for years, this devotional is sure to help you practically apply the power of God's Word to your daily life."

Ron Zappia, senior pastor and founder of Highpoint
Church, Naperville, IL; author of *The Marriage Knot*

"Warren Wiersbe speaks once again with the heart of a pastor, the skill of a scholar, the care of a mentor, and the love of a friend. His daily words of wisdom will nourish your soul, giving you a greater appreciation for biblical truth that applies to everyday life. Thank you, Warren, for inspiring and encouraging us with God's transformational truth."

Scott A. Poling, senior pastor at Harvest
New Beginnings Church, Oswego, IL

"Embark on a transformative journey with this 100-day devotional, *Becoming New*. Drawing from decades of Wiersbe's scholarly wisdom and Jacobsen's contemporary practical insight, it is a roadmap to spiritual growth. After encasing oneself daily in the spiritual fabric of the Word of God and prayer, readers emerge transformed—a testament to the power of faith and reverence. Dive in and discover the miraculous metamorphosis activated within these pages."

Robert Smith, PhD, Charles T. Carter Professor of Christian Preaching at Beeson Divinity School, author of *Exalting Jesus in Joshua*, *The Oasis of God*, and *Doctrine That Dances*

"Warren Wiersbe's timeless wisdom and profound insights into the heart of God are truly refreshing."

Philip Miller, senior pastor of The Moody Church

"In classic Wiersbe style, the foundation of each study is indisputably based upon and carefully linked to multiple key passages of Scripture. Since each timeless truth presented is firmly anchored in the immutable, God-breathed Word of God, the student who prayerfully delves into the teaching and studies the supporting passages will encounter the sincere milk of the Word, which satisfies the deepest thirst of the soul. I highly recommend this personal transformation guide."

Lawrence B. Windle, ThD, president of Rio Grande Bible Institute

"Classic Warren Wiersbe with a modern devotional twist. Whether you are a longtime fan of Dr. Wiersbe or discovering him for the first time, you will be encouraged and transformed as you spend 100 days walking though the story of Scripture from creation to Paul's arrival in Rome."

Adam Kipp, DMin, executive director of Rural Home Missionary Association

Warren W. Wiersbe

Edited by Dan Jacobsen

Becoming
NEW

100 Days of
Transformation
through God's Word

DAVID **C** COOK®

transforming lives together

BECOMING NEW
Published by David C Cook
4050 Lee Vance Drive
Colorado Springs, CO 80918 U.S.A.

Integrity Music Limited, a Division of David C Cook
Brighton, East Sussex BN1 2RE, England

DAVID C COOK® and related marks are registered trademarks of David C Cook.

Library of Congress Control Number 2024933398
ISBN 978-0-8307-8766-1
eISBN 978-0-8307-8767-8

© 2024 Scriptex, Inc.
Published in association with the literary agency of Mark Sweeney &
Associates, 302 Sherwood Drive, Carol Stream, IL 60188

The Team: Michael Covington, Stephanie Bennett, Jeff Gerke, Judy Gillispie,
Leigh Davidson, James Hershberger, Brian Mellema, Susan Murdock
Cover Design: Brian Mellema

Printed in the United States of America
First Edition 2024

1 2 3 4 5 6 7 8 9 10

080624

*To Carson, Evie, Nola, Nash, Lydia, Elin,
Miles, Graham, Ian, Ava, Ivy, Logan, Jack,
Makenna, Beau, and those who follow ...*

*May these words of old faith in the forever God
guide you to becoming new in Christ.*

CONTENTS

Part 2: In the New Testament

Preface

This is not a typical devotional book. It focuses on one theme—the daily transformation of your life and world through the truth of God given by the Holy Spirit of God. It does not cover every day of the year, but I trust that after you have studied and prayed your way through the book, you can give it to someone else for his or her renewal. Or start at the beginning and go through it again. The emphasis is not only on learning the Word but also loving the Word and living it in the power of the Holy Spirit.

Here is how to get the most help from this book:

- Read the main Scriptures noted for each day carefully and prayerfully. Meditate (think deeply) on them.
- Look up and read the Scriptures that are referenced within the daily reading! They are important to the development of each topic and provide enough context to be easily understood on their own. Much of the joy of this book comes from connecting the threads of larger themes.
- When the Spirit teaches you a truth, pause to give thanks and to ask the Lord to make it a reality in your life. Sudden impressions don't always last, so don't depend on them. Pray the truth into your mind and heart.

- Seek to obey that truth in your daily life. There will be both opportunities and obstacles, triumphs and temptations, but trust the Lord to see you through.
- Keep a prayer list.
- The applications at the end of each day's reading are an *opportunity*, not an assignment. Respond to one question or suggestion as your time permits.

As members of the body of Christ, we have the responsibilities of encouraging one another and building up one another in the faith, so share what God teaches you as the Lord directs. Please don't let learning spiritual truth inflate you with pride. "But while knowledge makes us feel important, it is love that strengthens the church" (1 Cor. 8:1). We must always "speak the truth in love, growing in every way more and more like Christ, who is the head of his body, the church" (Eph. 4:15).

You will find some truths repeated in these pages, not because I have nothing more to say but because these truths are important. The people who wrote the Bible occasionally repeated themselves for emphasis, and so did our Lord. May God bless you as you yourself experience the incredible transformation of "becoming new" and seek to share Christ's transforming truth with others.

Warren W. Wiersbe

A Note from the Editor

Warren Wiersbe was my grandfather. Throughout his life he wrote pro-lifically, such that when he died, nobody knew exactly *how many* books he'd written. The best estimates at the time put his total above 150 books. But as we began to cull through his files, it turned out that he had written more than were ever published, including this book you're holding now. It was unearthed in a dusty manila file folder, mostly completed but needing the work of an editor to pull it into final shape.

So for the better part of two years, I've worked with an archaeologist's approach: uncovering the treasures, preserving the structure, but also supply-ing missing pieces to bring the whole into view. Within this book are decades of biblical study, synthesized and distilled for any Christian to hold in his or her hands and grow in love for the Lord. These daily readings operate almost like a sage unpacking key texts of the Scriptures and showing "connective threads" present within the larger story of the Bible. By the time you're fin-ished with this book, Wiersbe will have unpacked for you the arc of Scripture in simple, easy-to-understand language.

A picture from nature helps illustrate the magnitude of wisdom found in these pages: Imagine a giant old sequoia tree standing tall in a forest. In its shadow grows a young sapling, and the two trees talk to each other. This book is the conversation between a giant of spiritual maturity and today's generation. The goal of this conversation is spiritual formation and growth in a life of blessing.

I heard my grandfather say on many occasions, "The church is always one generation away from extinction." I'm grateful he had this mindset, because he was concerned that we younger generations would know the Lord and be used in building His kingdom. He taught us the Word and prayed to that end. All of us are living links in the family of God, and it's brought me a lot of joy to finish this work to pass along these lessons to a new generation.

Throughout the journey I've taken in working with this project, I'm blessed to say I know my grandpa better. But more than that, I know Jesus better. And I hope, through your reading, you will too.

Dan Jacobsen

Part 1

Through the Old Testament

Day 1

Metamorphosis: How God Changes Us

Read Romans 11:33—12:2; 1 John 1:5–10

My first encounter with the word *metamorphosis* took place in Miss Gardner's fifth-grade science class when I was ten years old. She explained how caterpillars wrapped themselves in silk cocoons of their own weaving, waited for the right time, and came out as butterflies, and that this exciting process was called "metamorphosis." Why she used such a complicated word to explain "change" was a mystery to me until I encountered the word again in my first-year seminary Greek class, ten years later.

It is used four times in the New Testament: twice it describes our Lord's transfiguration (Matt. 17:2; Mark 9:2), and twice it refers to the changes Christians experience as they mature in their spiritual life (Rom. 12:2; 2 Cor. 3:18). Our Greek instructor explained that the word means "a permanent change on the outside that comes from the inside," and that was the definition I needed. All that the caterpillar needed to become a butterfly was already inside!

But we also learned that there is a Greek word that describes a *temporary* change that doesn't come from the inside. Our English equivalent would be "masquerade." If I put on a mask and a policeman's uniform and started writing tickets, I would be pretending and would probably be arrested for impersonating an officer. Satan's specialty is encouraging people to imitate the Christian life and not experience the "real thing." Satan himself even masquerades as an angel of light (2 Cor. 11:13–15). True Christians can experience change on the outside because they have the Holy Spirit within, who can bring out this miracle and make them more like Jesus (Rom. 8:29).

Among other things, the Bible is a record of the constant conflict in this world between illusion and reality, imitation on the outside and transformation from the inside. Satan is not a creator; he is a counterfeiter, offering people cheap imitations of the precious realities we have in Christ. Transformation is based on God's truth; imitation is based on Satan's lies (John 8:44). In 1 John 1:5–10, we are warned not to lie to others (vv. 5–7), to ourselves (vv. 8–9), or to God (v. 10).

The Scottish poet and novelist Sir Walter Scott wrote, "O what a tangled web we weave, / When first we practise to deceive!"[1] Believing Satan's lies will make us prisoners of illusion, but living by God's truth will make us free and keep us free (John 8:31–32, 44–45). Romans 12:2 commands us not to be conformed to this world but to be transformed (*metamorphosis*) from within by the renewing of our minds so that we will become more like Jesus Christ.

It is this wonderful day-by-day, step-by-step transformation experience that is the theme of this book. Our lives can be divine miracles or cheap imitations. The word translated "hypocrite" in the New Testament means "playactor, one who masquerades." We can choose to surrender to Jesus and enjoy reality or follow Satan and live in illusion. If we lie to others and to ourselves and if we try to lie to God, one day the truth will come out and the masquerade will be over.

Part of the process of change is dealing with our own self-deception. As we walk with the Lord through His Word, we must allow the truth to do its work in our hearts. God is in the business of taking counterfeits and converting them into the real thing. He will do this in you too, if you offer yourself—mind, body, and will—to God.

1. Are the words *truth* and *reality* part of your Christian vocabulary? How do you define these words?
2. Identify areas of your life that you need God to transform. Pray daily for God's Word and God's Spirit to change you from the inside out.

The Word of God

Read Genesis 1:1—2:3

The Bible opens with a description of divine transformation as God brought order out of chaos. Everything that transpired at creation began with God and depended on God. Jesus said, "For apart from me you can do nothing" (John 15:5). "For everything comes from him and exists by his power and is intended for his glory" (Rom. 11:36). While there are many elements at work in this miracle by which God brought about transformation, it's fitting to begin with the most repeated element: *the Word of God*.

In the first thirty-four verses of Genesis, we read "God said" ten times, "God called" three times, "God blessed" three times, and "God declared" one time. God spoke seventeen times! "The LORD merely spoke, and the heavens were created. He breathed the word, and all the stars were born.... For when he spoke, the world began! It appeared at his command" (Ps. 33:6, 9). Our spoken words don't possess this kind of sovereign authority, but if we believe God's promises and are led by the Holy Spirit, our weak words can release transformation power.

Whatever we do must be done by faith and in obedience to the will of God because "whatever is not from faith is sin" (Rom. 14:23 NASB1995). This means that what we do must be backed by the Word of God, for "faith comes from hearing, and hearing by the word of Christ" (Rom. 10:17 NASB1995). Faith is not an emotion that we work up but a gift the Spirit bestows as we live in His Word day by day. People in trouble who frantically turn the pages of the same Bible they've repeatedly ignored, yet now desperately look to for help, are not likely to find it. The believer who feeds on the Word *daily*, worships, prays to know God's will, and waits on the Lord will be given the right promises at the right time and can claim them by faith.

Three times in Scripture, Abraham is called God's friend (2 Chron. 20:7; Isa. 41:8; James 2:23) because he fellowshipped with God, listened to His Word, and obeyed His commands (Gen. 18:17–33; John 7:17). "The LORD is a friend to those who fear him. He teaches them his covenant" (Ps. 25:14). The worldly believer is God's enemy, not His friend (James 4:4), and so is the believer who lives to satisfy the old sinful nature (Rom. 8:5–8). The Word of God is "alive and powerful" (Heb. 4:12), and when we believe it, obey it, and act upon it, it will transform our lives and empower us to be transformers to God's glory (Matt. 17:19–21).

It has well been said that faith is not believing in spite of evidence but obeying in spite of consequence. We don't have to preach great sermons or perform miracles to be transformers. What we must do is yield to God, feed on His Word, pray, and obey when God shows us what to do—all of this in spite of feelings, circumstances, opposition, or consequences. "For we live by believing and not by seeing" (2 Cor. 5:7).

The people of this world stumble along from illusion to illusion as they walk by sight, but the people of God are transformed as they walk by faith in the Word of God. "For whatever is born of God overcomes the world. And this is the victory that has overcome the world—our faith" (1 John 5:4 NKJV).

1. Review the days of creation, and note the amazing results when God spoke. This same power resides in God's Word. Do you *want* God's power to transform you?

2. Evaluate your attitude toward the written Word of God. Are you skeptical? Arguing? Doubtful? Trusting? Obeying?

Day 3

The Spirit of God

Read Genesis 1:1–2; Psalm 104:24–32; John 14:16–20

When we mention the Persons in the Holy Trinity, we must be sure to use the little word *and* because it connects equals: "in the name of the Father *and* the Son *and* the Holy Spirit" (Matt. 28:19). Each member of the Trinity has specific ministries to perform in our lives individually and in the church collectively, but all three Persons work together to accomplish the divine plan. The Son came to glorify the Father, and the Spirit to glorify the Son (John 14:13; 16:14; 17:1). We are to love God, worship the Son, and walk by the Spirit.

In Genesis 1, the Holy Spirit is pictured as a bird hovering over the formlessness, emptiness, and darkness of the chaos. One of my seminary professors used to remind us that it was the ministry of the Holy Spirit to bring order out of chaos—in this world, in the church, and in the lives of God's people. I have seen this transformation take place as believers grew in their devotional life, established new priorities and goals, and experienced victories through the Spirit's power. No matter how chaotic a person's life might be, if he or she will yield to the Spirit, He will use the Word and prayer to bring cleansing and renewal. The Spirit teaches us and transforms us as we receive the Word within and act upon it (John 16:12–15).

The Lord's first action was to bring light into the darkness, which is also His first action when we trust Jesus Christ: "For God, who said, 'Let there be light in the darkness,' has made this light shine in our hearts so we could know the glory of God that is seen in the face of Jesus Christ" (2 Cor. 4:6). The record of creation goes on to tell us that God then transformed everything by *forming* and *filling*. In the first three days, He separated light from darkness, the waters beneath from the sky above, and the land from the waters. In the next three days, He filled up what had been created. On the fourth day, He put the heavenly bodies in place, and on the fifth day, the birds in the sky and the aquatic creatures in the waters. On the sixth day, He put the land animals and humans in their places. The Holy Spirit follows a similar pattern today: first He forms us; then He fills us. He wants each of us to be "a vessel for honor, sanctified, useful to the Master, prepared for every good work" (2 Tim. 2:21 NASB1995).

Older translations of the Bible use "Holy Ghost" rather than "Holy Spirit." The word "ghost" comes from the Old English word *geist*, meaning "spirit." I once heard a preacher call Him "the Holy Guest." But the Spirit is not a temporary guest; He is God permanently living in us (John 14:16; 1 Cor. 6:19). Someone has said that the Spirit is not just "resident"; He is "president." He is in charge! We must not grieve Him (Eph. 4:30), lie to Him (Acts 5), or stifle Him (1 Thess. 5:19). He is Christ's gift to us to minister as Jesus ministered to His disciples. We must keep on good terms with the Holy Spirit if we want to worship correctly (Eph. 5:18–20), use our spiritual gifts (1 Cor. 12), bear fruit (Gal. 5:22–23), get victory (Rom. 8:13), live in freedom (Gal. 5:13, 16), and understand the Scriptures (John 16:12–15). "Since we live by the Spirit, let us keep in step with the Spirit" (Gal. 5:25 NIV).

1. Which image of the Holy Spirit resonates with you today?
2. Considering the final paragraph, are you walking by the Spirit?

Day 4

The Image of God

Read Genesis 1:24–31; Psalm 8; Hebrews 2:5–9

Since God is spirit (John 4:24), He doesn't have a body, which means that being created in "the image of God" has nothing to do with our physical appearance. When the inspired authors of the Bible wrote about the eyes, ears, hands, or feet of the Lord, they were using human analogies to teach divine truths. "Made in God's image" has to do mainly with our spiritual nature and personality. God gave each of us a mind for thinking, a will for making decisions, and a heart to feel and express emotions. We also have a spirit within that enables us to fellowship with God and worship Him.

Compared with God, we humans are nothing, and we marvel that He pays any attention to us at all. "What are mere mortals that you should think about them, human beings that you should care for them?" (Ps. 8:4). God gave our first parents authority to "rule over the fish of the sea and over the birds of the sky and over the cattle and over all the earth, and over every creeping thing that creeps on the earth" (Gen. 1:26 NASB1995). God gave Adam and Eve dominion over His creation, but they lost it when they disobeyed His command. When Jesus, the last Adam (1 Cor. 15:45), came to earth, He exercised the dominion the first Adam lost (Heb. 2:5–8; Ps. 8:4–6). He had authority over the birds (Matt. 26:34, 69–75), the fish (Luke 5:1–11; Matt. 17:24–27; John 21:1–6), and the animals (Mark 1:12–13; 11:1–7), and they all obeyed Him.

Some people so emphasize the depravity of humankind that they are prone to forget the dignity of our being made in God's image and able to fellowship with Him. God supervises our prenatal development (Ps. 139:13–18), and after our birth, He "gives life and breath ... and he satisfies every need" (Acts 17:25; see also Ps. 144:3–4). He generously supplies sunshine and rain (Matt. 5:45) and considers us far more valuable than the birds and beasts (Matt. 6:26; 12:11–12). He loves us so much that He sent His Son as a human to die for us and save us (1 John 4:14). We are born sinners, but we can be born again through faith in Jesus and begin to grow in the image of God. Yes, we are sinners, but we are created in the image of God.

Because we bear the image of God and have trusted in Jesus for salvation, we have great hope and encouragement for the future. We are "citizens of heaven" (Phil. 3:20; see also Luke 10:20), and Jesus is preparing a home for us there (John 14:1–6). When our Lord returns, "He will take our weak mortal bodies and change them into glorious bodies like his own" (Phil. 3:21). "But we do know that we will be like him, for we will see him as he really is" (1 John 3:2). Meanwhile, it's our privilege and responsibility to be transformed here and now and become more like our Lord. We may also become transformers and let Him use us to introduce people to Jesus.

Public officials are frequently told by their promoters to improve their "image," but if they do improve, it's only a temporary change and part of the world's masquerade. True and lasting "image improvement" must come from within, through the work of the Holy Spirit. That's the only image worth having as He makes us more and more like Jesus.

1. In the tension between being created in the image of God and our fallen sinfulness, which describes how you think of yourself most?
2. How does seeing how you're made in the image of God influence your relationship with God, others, and yourself?

Day 5

The Rest of God

Read Genesis 2:1–3; Matthew 11:25—12:14; Hebrews 4:1–13

The whole Godhead models the rhythms of work and rest. "Let's go off by ourselves to a quiet place and rest awhile," Jesus told His disciples (Mark 6:31). If we are to serve effectively, work must be balanced with rest, and the noise and bustle of the crowd with quietness and solitude. God's plan includes four different "rests" for us to appreciate and appropriate.

Rest after work. God rested after creation, not because He was weary (Isa. 40:28) but because His work was completed. He gave Israel the seventh day as a day of physical rest. It was Adam's sin that turned work into sweat and toil (Gen. 3:17–19), and in spite of today's "labor-saving technology," we still need relief from the pressure and pain of work. God gave the Sabbath day to Israel to remind them that He is the Creator (Ex. 20:8–11; Neh. 9:13–14). All Ten Commandments except the fourth are repeated in the Epistles for believers today, but Colossians 2:16–17 and Romans 14 teach us not to judge one another with respect to special days. However, we must not ignore the principle behind the fourth commandment: we must be good stewards of our bodies and our time.

Rest after warfare. The phrase "place of rest" is used to describe the land God promised to Israel (Deut. 12:8–11; Josh. 1:15). It's unfortunate that tradition equates the crossing of the Jordan and the conquest of Canaan to the believer's death and entrance into heaven, when it really illustrates believers today dying to the old life and claiming their spiritual inheritance in Christ (Heb. 4:1–13). The only sword we use is "the sword of the Spirit, which is the word of God" (Eph. 6:17; see also John 18:36). Israel entered their rest by winning battles and claiming the land.

Rest in the midst of work and warfare. Our Lord's invitation in Matthew 11:28–30 promises to give rest to sinners who come to Him in faith. But we may also "find rest" as daily we learn of Him and yield to Him. During His ministry, Jesus helped people, taught His disciples, listened to false accusations, witnessed unbelief, and watched the opposition grow. Yet He was always in control and not upset by the enemy. On the eve of His arrest, He was able to say to His disciples, "I am leaving you with a gift—peace of mind and heart. And the peace I give is a gift the world cannot give. So don't be troubled or afraid" (John 14:27). This is "God's peace, which exceeds anything we can understand" (Phil. 4:7). The world gets periods of peace by diversion and distraction, but believers receive peace by transformation. Jesus compared our trials to the pains of a mother about to give birth (John 16:20–22): the same child that gives the mother pain also gives her joy! If we don't have peace and joy in the midst of our burdens and battles, we will become complaining drudges and never experience the joy of the Lord, which is our strength (Neh. 8:10).

Rest eternal. We have an eternal rest before us in heaven (Heb. 4:9; Rev. 14:13). Jesus is preparing a rest for His people (John 14:1–6) where we will worship, minister, learn, and bring glory to God. Read Revelation 21–22 and find rest for your soul.

1. Does the rhythm of your life allow you space to be a human "being" (who takes time to rest), or would you define yourself more as a human "doing" (who refuses to rest)?
2. Is your soul at rest (Matt. 11:28–30)?

Day 6

The Enemy of God

Read Genesis 3; 2 Corinthians 11:12–15

All true believers in Jesus Christ battle three insidious enemies: the world around us, the old nature within us, and the devil and his demonic armies who are against us (Eph. 2:1–10; 6:10–18). The devil is a fallen angel (Isa. 14:12–14) who wants to be like God so he can receive worship (Matt. 4:8–11), and many people unwittingly *do* worship Satan. He uses the pressures of the world and the flesh to make us into conformers because he doesn't want us to be transformers and defeat him (Rom. 12:1–2).

Satan is an imitator and a deceiver, a liar and a destroyer (John 8:44; Rev. 9:11). In Genesis 3, he is a serpent who deceives (2 Cor. 11:1–4), and in Genesis 4, he is a lion who devours and destroys (1 Pet. 5:8). Satan can appear as one of God's angels just as his human agents can appear as servants of God (2 Cor. 11:12–14; Matt. 7:15) and his followers as children of God (1 John 3:12; Matt. 13:24–30, 36–43). Satan can perform counterfeit miracles to deceive the world (2 Thess. 2:9; Rev. 13). He is a formidable adversary.

When Satan tempted Eve, he masqueraded as one of God's creatures and deceived her. First he questioned God's word, asking, "Did God really say?" Then he denied God's word, asserting, "You will not die!" Finally, he substituted his own lie when he told Eve, "You will be like God." He suggested that the Lord was holding out on them and used the same tactic when he tempted Jesus. "The Father called You His 'beloved Son.' If He loves You, why are You hungry? Why does He make You fast? You have the power to change stones into bread, so why not do it?" Once we question God's Word and God's love, we start to feel sorry for ourselves and decide we deserve what the Devil offers us.

Eve was deceived by the Devil, but Adam sinned deliberately with his eyes wide open (1 Tim. 2:14). He chose to stay with his wife, now a sinner, rather than obey the Lord, and this is why it is Adam who caused the fall of the race (Rom. 5:12–21). Jesus is called "the last Adam" (1 Cor. 15:45) because, in contrast to the first Adam, He obeyed the Father, died for our sins, and rescued us from Satan's dominion. "Just as everyone dies because we all belong to Adam, everyone who belongs to Christ will be given new life" (1 Cor. 15:22).

Christians have in Jesus Christ adequate protection from Satan and his demons as well as provision for victory over temptation. Read Matthew 4:1–11, and note that Jesus didn't carry on a conversation with the Enemy but used the sword of the Spirit to defeat him: "It is written!" (Cross-reference Heb. 4:12 and Ps. 119:11 to see the link.) Note also that He was filled with the Spirit before Satan appeared. As we begin each day, we must put on the armor by faith, piece by piece (Eph. 6:10–18), and trust the Holy Spirit to empower us and help us use the Word.

We must spend time in the Word each day, preferably in the morning, for often the Lord gives us in the morning just the promise or warning we will need during the day. Don't depend on your circumstances to rescue you; Satan tempted Eve in Paradise and Jesus when He was on the highest point of the temple! Claim the promise of 1 Corinthians 10:13, and the Lord will help you win the victory, and that victory will make it easier to win the next battle. "But in all these things we overwhelmingly conquer through Him who loved us" (Rom. 8:37 NASB1995).

1. Are your daily rhythms and routines enabling you to fight the schemes and lies of the Enemy? Begin today the habit of praying on the armor of God as you prepare for the day (Eph. 6:10–18).

2. Take a moment now and pray for discernment to recognize the lies and deceptions of our enemy.

Day 7

The Promise of God

Read Genesis 9:8–17; Ezekiel 1; Revelation 4

I was surprised to hear that the song "Over the Rainbow" from *The Wizard of Oz* was named the "Song of the Twentieth Century."[1] Rarely does a song still garner attention six decades after it was written. The lyrics evoke a sense of hope for tomorrow that will be here soon. Rainbows have fascinated humanity since the beginning. Of course, the Bible has something to say about rainbows and the promise they hold for those who trust in God's redemptive, transforming plan.

God's grace—the certainty of His Word (Gen. 9:8–17). The rainbow was the sign of God's covenant with us that there would not be another flood to destroy all life upon the earth. We see dark clouds gather before the storm, and they are accompanied by lightning and thunder and sometimes strong wind, and the coming of a storm frightens people. But if they would recall the rainbow they saw after the last storm, their hearts would not be afraid. Charles Spurgeon points out that the bow is aimed upward, toward heaven, which suggests that the judgment for sin was aimed at God and not us![2] "The LORD laid on him [Jesus] the sins of us all" (Isa. 53:6). God has every right to destroy the wicked, yet He keeps His Word and calls sinners to repentance.

God's government—the mystery of His will (Ezek. 1). Ezekiel, a Jewish priest exiled in Babylon, was called to be a prophet. But exile wasn't his greatest burden, for the Lord showed him a storm, and in the midst of the storm, a crystal pavement carrying a throne. There were wheels at each corner of the pavement with an angelic creature guiding the workings of each wheel. On the throne was the Lord God, completely in charge. The vision revealed to Ezekiel that a terrible invasion would sweep over the kingdom of Israel and result in the devastation of the land, the ruin of Jerusalem, and the destruction of the holy temple. *But around the throne was a rainbow!* In His anger, the Lord was remembering mercy (Hab. 3:2). In the midst of life's storms, we know that God is on the throne, surrounded by a rainbow of grace, and He is at work weaving all things together for good for those who love Him (Rom. 8:28). We don't always understand God's workings, but we can always trust His will. Mysteries we cannot explain abound in our lives, but God is on His throne and we need not be discouraged.

God's greatness—the glory of His worship (Rev. 4). "And the glow of an emerald circled his throne like a rainbow" (v. 3). John recorded the many terrible judgments God would send on the earth, but God was on the throne and the rainbow assured His people the judgments would result in His glory. The judgments recorded in Revelation 6–18 climax with a heavenly "hallelujah chorus" (19:1–10). "Praise the LORD! For the Lord our God, the Almighty, reigns" (v. 6). Seeing the rainbow around the throne comforts and assures us as we worship the Lord in the splendor of His holiness (Ps. 96:9).

We may not see visions as did Ezekiel and John, but a promise in Scripture, a verse from a hymn, or even an encouraging word from a friend can be a "rainbow" to assure us that all is well. Noah reminds us that God's grace is present *after* the storm. Ezekiel reminds us that His government is present *during* the storm. And John reveals to us that His greatness is present *before* the storm! The cumulative effect is to remind us to trust in the Lord at all times.

1. Can you remember a storm in your life that you can look back upon and see the ever-present grace, government, and greatness of God?
2. Which of God's promises do you need to claim today?

The Glory of God

Read Exodus 40:34–38; Psalm 19

God created the universe to display His glory, but sinful humans "exchanged the glory of the incorruptible God for an image in the form of corruptible man and of birds and four-footed animals and crawling creatures" (Rom. 1:23 NASB1995). Humans worshipped the very creatures over which they were to have dominion and "traded the truth about God for a lie" (Rom. 1:25). In the Greek text, that verse more accurately reads "for *the* lie," which is worshipping and serving creation and not the Creator. Satan has always wanted to be worshipped (Isa. 14:14; Matt. 4:8–11), and he receives this worship when people worship idols or anything else that takes the place of God. Idols are not just small statues or images on a shelf or in a chapel. We can have idols in our minds and imaginations as well.

Everything about God is glorious, but He is glorified most when He is transforming people and situations in ways nobody else could match. *God's glory is the brilliance reflected by all His perfections and the honor given Him for His wise and gracious plan of salvation.* Idols have no transforming power, except to make people worse as they become like the false gods they worship (Ps. 115:1–8). Many people worship money and depend on it to provide goods and services, but money has no perfections and cannot of itself build character or change situations. "I am the LORD; that is my name! I will not give my glory to anyone else" (Isa. 42:8). The first request in the Lord's Prayer is that the name of God be honored (Matt. 6:9). This means we must not ask for anything that, if granted, would not glorify the Lord. God is glorified most when He does remarkable things that we cannot understand. We used to say at Youth for Christ, "If you can explain what's going on, God didn't do it!"

Other nations in Israel's time had sanctuaries, priests, sacrifices, and rituals, *but only the Jewish temple in Jerusalem was indwelt by the glory of God!* When Moses dedicated the tabernacle, God's glory moved in (Ex. 40), and when Solomon dedicated the temple, God's glory moved in (1 Kings 8:10–11). Whatever blessings we seek from the Lord, the most important one is that He be glorified in all that we have, are, and do.

Sometimes ministry itself can become an idol that robs God of glory. This old story serves as a cautionary tale: The pulpit of a certain church stood in front of a beautiful stained-glass window showing Jesus with outstretched arms, inviting sinners to come. One Sunday a guest preacher ministered, and a little boy asked his mother, "Mommy, where is the man who usually stands there so we can't see Jesus?" When we work for God without worshipping God, we can get in the way of people seeing the glory of God.

God is glorified when His Son is honored, and Jesus is honored when His people say and do what makes Him look great. Paul called this "Christ ... magnified in my body" (Phil. 1:20 NKJV). People think Jesus is "small" in this world compared to athletic stars and movie celebrities, so let's be like microscopes that make Him look bigger. They also think He is far away in the past, so let's be like telescopes that bring Him closer. We are like a lens, and the cleaner we are, the better they will be able to see our Lord.

Jesus sets the example: "I brought glory to you here on earth by completing the work you gave me to do" (John 17:4). There is work for us to do. Let's complete it for His glory!

1. God's glory is a constant in our lives, if we have eyes to see Him. What God-glorifying work has He done in your life? Have you praised Him for it?

2. Who have you shared that experience with, to further glorify God?

Day 9

God's Radiant Face

Read Numbers 6:22–27; Psalms 4 and 67

Children learn to "read" the faces of their parents and teachers and interpret what the various expressions mean. A smile means delight, a side-eye means caution, and a frown danger. The Jewish people understood the Lord's face to do the same. Whenever they said the Lord's face was "shining" or "smiling" upon them, it meant that God was pleased with His people and was blessing them, and when He hid His face, He was displeased and disciplining them (Pss. 13:1; 44:23–26; 89:46).

God covenanted to bless Israel with every earthly blessing they needed as long as the people obeyed Him, and He kept His promise. When they began to worship idols, He removed these blessings and put His people into bondage (Judg. 2:10–15). He has blessed His church today with "every spiritual blessing in the heavenly realms because we are united with Christ" (Eph. 1:3; see also 2 Pet. 1:3–4). As long as we walk in the light and obey the Lord, we can draw upon His blessings and experience a transformed life. To disobey means to walk in darkness and forfeit the sunshine of His love (1 John 1:5–10).

Marriage and parenthood are good illustrations of this truth. Marriage is a *union* that brings blessing and joy as long as there is *communion*. But if disagreement and distrust enter the home, the atmosphere becomes tense and there are no smiling faces. Disobedient children can look at their mother's face, see no smiles, and expect no special favors. The union isn't broken, but the family communion is, and it won't return until somebody says, "I'm sorry."

It's remarkable that the face of the Lord shines upon His obedient children even when everything around them is dark and depressing. Paul and Silas were beaten and thrown into a dark dungeon, but God's face smiled upon them, and they prayed and sang hymns, and God's light broke in (Acts 16:25). The Bible calls this experience "songs in the night" (Job 35:10; see also Ps. 42:8). Before He went out to Gethsemane, Jesus sang (Mark 14:26). "Everything is going against me," said Jacob (Gen. 42:36), when actually everything was working *for* him! Because we know God is for us (Rom. 8:31–32), it matters not who or what may be against us.

There's an old hymn called "God Holds the Key" that sums it up well:

> *I cannot read His future plans;*
> *But this I know:*
> *I have the smiling of His face,*
> *And all the refuge of His grace,*
> *While here below.*[1]

Everyone else may be frowning at us, but if we have "the smiling of His face," we can go forward, do our work for His glory, and hear Him say, "Well done."

1. God's grace means we do not earn God's smile; He always welcomes us into His presence. But our misperceptions can rob us: "Is God embarrassed by me? I'm such a failure. Jesus must be disappointed in me." God knows everything about us—and loves us.
2. What expression is on your spiritual face when you enter God's presence?

Day 10

The Glory of God in Us

Read Exodus 34:28–35; 2 Corinthians 3

Paul makes the amazing announcement that Christians today can have a "shining face experience" even greater than that of Moses. Consider the lessons these passages teach us.

There are no special people. We must never say, "If I were only a prophet like Moses, I could also have a great 'mountaintop experience' with the Lord." Although we all have different gifts and callings, God has no "favorites" and God's grace cares nothing about human merit. "There is no longer Jew or Gentile, slave or free, male and female. For you are all one in Christ Jesus" (Gal. 3:28). Every obedient and cleansed believer may come boldly into God's presence to worship and pray (Heb. 10:19–22). We all have the privilege of knowing God's will and, with His help, doing it for His glory. One day "they will each be rewarded according to their own labor" (1 Cor. 3:8 NIV).

There are no special places. "The Most High doesn't live in temples made by human hands" (Acts 7:48), nor does He meet with us on fiery mountains (Heb. 12:18–24). While we may have meaningful memories associated with special places, simply being in these places does not duplicate past experiences. While we may have deeply emotional feelings as we remember what God has done, those feelings may prevent us from moving into a new thing God has for us. It isn't necessary for us to find a "holy place," because God knows our needs and can meet them anywhere.

There are no exclusive blessings. Not all opportunities and blessings are given to everyone, but we will be judged according to what *we* have done with what God gave *us* and not what others have done with what He gave them (Matt. 25:14–30). God chooses His workers and uses them according to His sovereign will, but all His children have been blessed with everything they need to live for God and serve Him (1 Cor. 12:4–6; Eph. 1:3; 2 Pet. 1:3–4). God knows what is best for us.

Our blessings are greater. Paul explains that God wrote the law on tablets of stone but today He writes His Word on our hearts (2 Cor. 3:1–3). The process of *becoming new* begins not on the outside but rather in our hearts! "Guard your heart above all else, for it determines the course of your life" (Prov. 4:23). The old covenant of law brought death, but the new covenant brings life (2 Cor. 3:4–8). The glory at Sinai is gone, and the glory on Moses's face faded away, but the glory we receive grows greater (2 Cor. 3:9–11). Moses wore a veil so the people could not see the glory fading away (2 Cor. 3:12–15), but we have nothing to hide!

Where you look influences what you become. As the children of God look into the mirror of the Word of God (James 1:22–25), they see Jesus and are transformed into His image, "from glory to glory" (2 Cor. 3:18 KJV). The average person at Sinai couldn't have had the experience Moses had, but *we* can—and we should! Moses didn't know his face was aglow, nor will you see your face shine as you fellowship with the Lord, but others will see it and take note. And as our faces glow (especially in times of pain), others will be attracted to Jesus (Matt. 5:14–16).

1. For our lives to reflect God's glory, we must invest time in His presence. When Peter and John publicly defended

the faith, their critics "recognized them as men who had been with Jesus" (Acts 4:13). Can others note that you have been with Jesus?

2. What are some dangers of comparing ourselves to other Christian servants?

Day 11

The Ways of God

Read Psalms 23 and 32

The Lord could have spoken one word and instantly brought the entire universe into existence, but He chose to do His work on six successive days. There is a lesson in this truth: *God takes His time.* God created planet earth to operate on a twenty-four-hour schedule, which means we must live a day at a time. Moses reminded the Israelites, "You have six days each week for your ordinary work" (Ex. 20:9), and Jesus taught us to pray, "Give us this day our daily bread" (Matt. 6:11 NASB1995). Creation operates a day at a time, and so should we (Matt. 6:25–34). When our Lord served here on earth, He followed a daily schedule ordained by the Father (Isa. 50:4; John 1:29, 35, 43; 2:1, 4), and this is a good example for us to follow.

God isn't in a hurry, but most people are, and they pay for it dearly. They fill their schedules with reminders of events to attend, people to meet, and jobs to do, rarely stopping to ask if all this activity is really accomplishing anything. We rarely say, "If the Lord wants us to ..." (see James 4:13–17), but rush from one appointment to another, secretly pleased that we aren't "wasting" time. Jesus was never in a hurry because of an overcrowded schedule, and yet He always accomplished each day's assignment (John 9:4; 7:30; 8:20; 12:23, 27; 13:1; 17:1).

In Psalm 32:8–9, King David warns us against two extremes: being stubborn like the mule or impulsive like the horse. When David sinned with

Bathsheba, he was impulsive like the horse, and when for nearly a year he refused to confess his sins, he was stubborn like the mule. Moses impulsively killed a man in Egypt and fled to Midian, but when he was called to go to Egypt to liberate his people, Moses argued with the Lord and acted like a mule. God's people are sheep, and following the Good Shepherd, Jesus Christ, is the best way to live. The believer who says, "Into Your hand I commit my spirit…. My times are in Your hand" (Ps. 31:5, 15 NASB1995), is sure to make the best use of each day.

Our Father in heaven always gives His best to those who leave the choice to Him. "The counsel of the LORD stands forever, the plans of His heart to all generations" (Ps. 33:11 NKJV). The will of God for you comes from His heart and is an expression of His love for you. We may not understand how an emergency operation or an auto accident can express God's love, but we don't live on explanations—we live on promises. We walk by faith and learn to say "Thank You, Lord" even when we hurt or when we are weary.

We are not horses or mules. "We are his people, the sheep of his pasture" (Ps. 100:3). When we follow the Shepherd, we are safe and lack nothing we need. We live a day at a time. In the morning, the Shepherd leads us into the pastures and then back to the fold each evening, and He cares for our every need. If one of the sheep goes astray, the Shepherd seeks it and brings it back. In the Old Testament, every Passover the sheep died for the shepherds, but at Calvary, the Shepherd died for the sheep (John 10:11).

God's ways are to be trusted and walked in. Like David, say to God right now, "The LORD is my shepherd; I have all that I need" (Ps. 23:1).

1. Do you need to make any adjustments to keep in step with the Shepherd's pace and plan for your life?

2. Time is a gift and a treasure. It can become a tyrant. Are you content to accomplish what God intends, in a day's time?

Day 12

Living Links in God's Plan

Read Genesis 5

Satan's attack against the human race didn't stop God's plans to redeem His creation, for He gave Adam and Eve another son, whom they named Seth (Gen. 4:25–26). Frequently in the Old Testament you find the Lord replacing the firstborn with another son, teaching us that God rejects our first birth and tells us we must be born again (John 3:1–17). Ishmael was Abraham's firstborn son, but Isaac took his place, and Isaac's firstborn, Esau, was replaced by Jacob. Jacob's firstborn by Leah was Reuben, but he was replaced by Joseph, his firstborn son by Rachel. Joseph's firstborn was Manasseh, but he was replaced by Ephraim. "You must be born again" (John 3:7). This genealogy teaches us some valuable lessons.

The sad consequences of one sin. The phrase "and then he died" is found eight times in this chapter, "for the wages of sin is death" (Rom. 6:23). There is "a time to be born and a time to die" (Eccl. 3:2), and we don't know when our time to die will come. The certainty of death is one of the most important facts of life, yet society does all it can to avoid that fact and to camouflage it when it does happen. Death is an enemy (1 Cor. 15:26) that must be faced honestly, and the only way to be prepared is by trusting in Jesus Christ (John 11:25–26). But the reality of death ought to motivate us to make the most of life by obeying the Lord (Ps. 90:12).

The great value of one person. The names of Adam, Methuselah, and Noah are familiar to most people, but the rest are probably strangers, yet each one of them is a "living link" in God's gracious plan of salvation. Every genealogy in the Bible reminds us that the promise of the Redeemer (Gen. 3:15) was fulfilled through the Jewish nation, and each "living link" was important. From generation to generation, God was watching and overruling and accomplishing His will. In spite of satanic opposition and human frailty and failure, the hour arrived when the Son of God came into the world to save sinners!

The encouragement of one good example. Enoch is the only person in the genealogy of whom it could not be said "and then he died." God took him bodily to heaven (Gen. 5:21–24)! The world was so devoted to wickedness in Enoch's day that God finally had to send a flood to destroy civilization and make a new beginning with Noah and his family. Enoch boldly proclaimed the truth (Jude 14–15) as he lived a godly life and pleased God (Heb. 11:5). One day God's people on earth will be taken to heaven, and we want to live as though it might happen today (1 Thess. 4:13–18; 1 John 2:28—3:3).

The universal presence of one desire (Gen. 5:28–32). That one desire is *rest*. Society was wicked (Gen. 6:1–8, 11–13), life was burdensome (Gen. 3:14–19), and death was always hovering. A change in circumstances could not bring rest; that can come only from faith in Jesus Christ (Matt. 11:28–30). The name Noah means "rest" or "comfort," and through Noah, God gave a new beginning. The water that buried the earth buoyed up the ark, giving us a picture of death, burial, and resurrection—a picture of what Jesus did for us! No one will find peace until they submit to Jesus, trust Him, and obey His Word. "I am leaving you with a gift—peace of mind and heart," said Jesus (John 14:27). If you have accepted that gift, you've become a living link in God's plan. Who's after you?

1. Who did God use in your life to link you into the family of God?

2. Who in your family are you praying will know, love, and follow God?

Day 13

Abraham: The Founding Father

Read Genesis 12–13; Hebrews 11:8–19

If scriptwriters or studio executives had written the beginning of God's world-changing plan of salvation, they would never have chosen two elderly people like Abraham and Sarah as original cast members. They were too old to have children, they did not know the true and living God, and they worshipped idols in the pagan city of Ur (Josh. 24:2). Furthermore, God made them wait twenty-five years from His promise to His provision of a son. People want things done quickly these days! But God is never in a hurry, His timing is always right (Gal. 4:4), and He has a plan.

The Lord graciously revealed Himself to Abraham (Acts 7:2), who shared the good news with Sarah, and by faith they left Ur to go to the land God would show them. "He went without knowing where he was going" (Heb. 11:8; see also Gen. 15:7). They were to be the "foundation stones" of the nation of Israel, which would bring salvation to the world (John 4:22). Their son Isaac would be the caretaker of the family, Isaac's son Jacob would build the family, and his son Joseph would protect and provide for the nation. God has His plans and, when we walk by faith, He works everything out in His way and His time. Abraham models what it means to live by faith.

We live by faith when we receive God's Word and obey it. Abraham didn't have a complete Bible, but he did have God's promise of guidance, care, and protection (Gen. 12:1–3). God's people today have the written

Word of God and ought to be able to discern God's will. To ignore the Bible and attempt to know God's will and serve Him is foolish and can be disastrous.

We live by faith when we worship God and know His character. Wherever Abraham and Sarah went, Abraham built an altar to the Lord, worshipped Him, and came to better understand God's character. Abraham also pitched his tent and said to his neighbors that he was a pilgrim and stranger. Abraham was a wealthy man and could have built a fine house and settled down, but that wasn't God's plan for his life. You and I today may say we live in permanent structures, but do we? Paul says we live in tents (2 Cor. 5:1–5)! Once we stop feeling "temporary" and start "settling down," our walk of faith starts to waver and then weaken (Heb. 11:8–10).

We live by faith when we depend on God's power. How could an old couple like Abraham and Sarah ever have a child? By the resurrection power of God (Heb. 11:11–12; Rom. 4:16–21). Faith is living without scheming. Each time Abraham and Sarah made their own plans—fleeing to Egypt, lying about Sarah, Abraham marrying Hagar—it only caused trouble. And when God tested Abraham's faith, Abraham agreed to slay his son Isaac because he believed God could raise Isaac from the dead (Heb. 11:17–19).

Three times in Scripture, Abraham is called "the friend of God" (2 Chron. 20:7; Isa. 41:8; James 2:23). His nephew Lot was "a friend of the world" and therefore an enemy of God (James 4:1–6). Friends speak and listen to each other, open their hearts to each other, and seek the very best for each other. They also can be silent while enjoying each other's companionship. Abraham kept his eyes on the heavenly city (Heb. 11:13–16; 12:1–2). Keep your eyes fixed on the heavenly city, by faith.

1. In the retrospective of your life, in what ways will your friends and family say that you, like Abraham, "believed God"?

2. God calls us to live on promises, not explanations. Journeying through these one hundred days of becoming new is a great way to embrace God's promises in your life. Which promise are you grateful for today?

Day 14

Isaac: The Exemplary Father

Read Genesis 22:1–19; 27:1–40

It has often been pointed out that Isaac's name is frequently sandwiched between the names of his famous father, Abraham, and his famous son Jacob, while he himself claims no fame. But in his miraculous birth (Gen. 18:1–15), his loving obedience on Mount Moriah (Gen. 22), and his marriage to Rebekah (Gen. 24), he is a beautiful picture of our Lord Jesus Christ. Even more, Galatians 4:28 tells us that all believers in Jesus Christ are "children of the promise, just like Isaac." Like Isaac, we have experienced a miraculous birth, a spiritual one, and we have been born free and wealthy as part of a very special family.

This is what makes Isaac a great example to us today. Isaac wasn't a pioneer of faith like Abraham or a hardworking servant like Jacob, but he fulfilled the purpose God assigned to him. He was a living link between the founder and the builder of the nation of Israel. Never underestimate the ministry or the importance of those God has made caretakers, for without their faithful stewardship, His work cannot go on.

We are prone to magnify the exceptional and minimize what we call "the ordinary," but God never takes that approach. *Every member of the body has an important function, and so does every worker in the field, whether plowing, sowing, watering, weeding, or harvesting.* We will discover at the judgment seat of Christ that the believers we may have underrated really had important ministries we knew nothing about. I read about a church organist whose concert was introduced with oratory, but when he sat down to play, the keys made no music. Then he remembered that the boy who kept the bellows working was not even recognized. (Organs worked differently in a prior era.) He apologized to the boy and thanked him before the whole congregation, and then there was music.

I have pastored three churches and served on the staffs of two ministry organizations, as well as on several boards, and I know that the real heroes of "the work" aren't necessarily the people named on the official stationery or seen on the platform. Some of the most important workers in most local churches are the facility managers who keep the buildings working, the volunteers who offer their precious time and energy, and the office staff who free up the ministers so they can help the people. To the Lord, no service is "ordinary." Even giving a cup of cold water to a thirsty person is not an "ordinary" act to the Lord (Matt. 25:35–40). Before He began His three years of ministry, Jesus worked for years in a carpenter shop, which pleased His Father (Matt. 3:13–17). Later, Jesus took ordinary water and turned it into extraordinary wine (John 2:1–11) and a little boy's ordinary lunch and fed more than five thousand people (John 6:1–15).

God doesn't classify organizations or people as "ordinary" and "special," or "secular" and "sacred." No matter who we are or what He tells us to do, we are to do everything to the glory of God (1 Cor. 10:31). Isaac was a quiet caretaker, a family link between Abraham the founder and Jacob the builder. If people take you and your work for granted, don't get discouraged. God might be using you in ways only generations from now will recognize.

1. Are you a pastor who has benefited from the "behind the scenes" service of congregants? Take a moment to thank God for them. Are you a caretaker in your family? Take a moment to thank God for your opportunity to minister.

2. There are no small places and no small ministries. Your work is important to the family of God, to the community around you, and to the Lord, regardless of recognition. Ask God for eyes to see the work He has prepared in advance for you (Eph. 2:10).

Day 15

Jacob: The Wrestling Father

Read Genesis 25:19–34; 28:10–22; 32:22–31

When we think of radical transformations, Jacob's story certainly tops the list. It would be easy for us to criticize Jacob and mock his failures, yet he was the man God used to father the twelve sons who gave the world the twelve tribes of Israel. Like all of us, Jacob had his faults. He deceived his father and his brother, Esau, but he was also a sacrificing, hardworking man of faith. For twenty years, he labored and sacrificed to please his scheming father-in-law, Laban, who from time to time cheated him. Jacob married four wives and had to provide for them and thirteen children, and yet he didn't give up.

The Lord has deigned to call Himself "the God of Jacob" and "the God of Israel" (Jacob's new name), which ought to be enough recommendation for us. Jacob called God "the Mighty One of Jacob … the Shepherd, the Rock of Israel" (Gen. 49:24). If the Lord had to use only perfect people, He would never get His work done, for there are no perfect people. In spite of Jacob's deceptions and maneuverings, God used him, blessed him, and made him a blessing. God does this because He loves us and has gifted and assigned each of His children to do the work He has chosen for them (Eph. 2:10).

Each experience Jacob had helped to mold him and make him a man of God. He fled from home to escape the anger of his brother and walked right into a household headed by Laban, who worshipped idols and could out-scheme Jacob. I heard about a man who read online that most auto accidents occurred within five miles of home, so he told his family they were going to move! Of course, a change in geography will never solve your problems. We might be able to run away from our enemies, but we always take our biggest enemy—ourselves—along with us.

God met Jacob at Bethel and promised to care for him (Gen. 28:13–15). When Jacob was returning home, he wrestled with the Lord at Peniel (Gen. 32:22–31). God gave him a limp and also a new name—Israel, "a prince with God." Often God has to break us before He can make us, not because He is weak but because we are too strong. For the rest of his days, that limp reminded Jacob that he had to decide which of his names would control his life: Jacob "the schemer" or Israel "the prince with God."

God prevailed over Jacob in order to protect him from Esau. Then later, Jacob experienced problems with his ten oldest sons, especially when they lied about his favorite son, Joseph. In one sense, Jacob was being repaid for what he had done to his own father and brother, but God prevailed once more and saved the whole family. Jacob had seventeen years of rest and comfort in Egypt, blessed (and scolded) his sons before he died, and died just as he had lived—a pilgrim, leaning on his staff (Gen. 32:10; Heb. 11:21).

In the final analysis, Jacob's life was one wrestling match after another. Yet he changed for the better when he refused to let go of his struggle with God. After seeing the face of God (Gen. 32:22–31), Jacob became a new man with a new walk and a new name. Jacob's name is forever honored in our Lord's genealogy (Matt. 1:2; Luke 3:34). He suffered greatly, yet the Lord worked everything out for good (Gen. 50:20). Jacob never read Romans 8:28, but he certainly experienced it and makes it real to us today.

1. The world tells us that people don't change. But Jacob became new! How does this encourage you?

2. Are you wrestling with God about an issue or incident? What does Jacob's experience with God tell you about the process that God might be taking you on toward becoming new?

Day 16

Joseph: The Dreaming Father

Read Genesis 37 and 45; Psalm 105:16–22

The biblical account of Joseph begins with a pampering father and ten angry brothers whose hatred for Joseph almost led to murder. There were two things that infuriated them: he was his father's favorite and wore a beautiful garment to prove it, and he dreamed twice that the family would all bow down to him. Joseph's brothers sold him to be a slave in Egypt. Potiphar, one of Pharaoh's officers, eventually put Joseph in charge of his household affairs. Potiphar's wife repeatedly tried to seduce Joseph but failed. When her lust turned to hatred, she lied about him and had him thrown into the dungeon. He interpreted the dreams of two prisoners, and they came true.

Later, when Pharaoh had some perplexing dreams, Joseph interpreted them and so impressed Pharaoh that he made Joseph second ruler in the land. During the terrible famine that Pharaoh's dreams predicted, Joseph's older brothers traveled to Egypt twice to get food, and Joseph so managed things that they were finally brought to repentance and did bow to him. Joseph told them to bring their father and their families to Egypt, and there he cared for them. Joseph the hated brother became their provider and protector, and the people of Israel increased rapidly and became a nation. Now, let's glean some spiritual truths from this remarkable story.

Believe what the Lord tells you. Joseph had no written word from the Lord such as we have today, so God spoke to him in dreams, as He did with Pharaoh. God told Joseph that one day he would be a powerful ruler and his brothers would bow down to him. It was this revelation from God that encouraged Joseph and kept him going those many years away from home. There were days when his burdens were heavy, but he kept trusting God in spite of his circumstances.

Know that the Lord is with you. When Joseph was taken to Egypt, God was with him, and when he went to work at Potiphar's house, God continued to be with him (Gen. 39:2–3). Even when he was thrown into the dungeon, God was with him (Gen. 39:21, 23). No matter the circumstances or situations, transformed people will transform things. Joseph was the finest worker not only in Potiphar's house but also in the prison, and because he was faithful in a few things, God eventually made him ruler over many things (Matt. 25:21). All these events helped to mature Joseph, preparing him for greater things.

Wait on the Lord's timing. Joseph was seventeen when he was taken to Egypt and thirty when he became the second ruler of the land, which means thirteen years passed before he got his freedom. Then another seven years passed before his family was reconciled to him. For twenty long years, Joseph waited for his dreams to be fulfilled, because it is through "faith and endurance" that we inherit what God has promised (Heb. 6:12; see also Rom. 5:3–5).

Let God transform you. During those years of suffering, Joseph became more like our Lord Jesus Christ. He was rejected by his brethren, was sold, and suffered unjustly. He wept over his brethren. He was beloved of his father. He went from suffering to glory. He forgave those who sinned against him. While rejected by his own, he took a Gentile bride. The major difference is that Joseph died a normal death and ended up in a coffin (Gen. 50:26), while Jesus died a cruel death and after three days arose from the dead. God didn't waste Joseph's years or dreams. Waiting, trusting, and believing God is how He makes us new!

1. Genesis 50:20 summarizes what Joseph learned in God's transforming process. Memorize it!
2. How have you experienced God's power to turn evil into good?

Day 17

Israel: The Nation of Fathers

Read Genesis 49:1–28; Revelation 5

Please don't think that the scene described in Genesis 49 is a picture of the future judgment seat of Christ, where our works will be judged and our service rewarded (Rom. 14:10–13; 2 Cor. 5:10). Jacob dealt with the past sins of three sons, but God tells us that He will remember our sins no more (Jer. 31:34; Heb. 8:12; 10:17). Jacob the patriarch was simply settling unfinished family business and announcing the future of the twelve tribes. At the same time, he brought encouragement and news about a future Redeemer.

Jacob began with the horrific rewards of sin (Gen. 49:1–7). Reuben, the firstborn, should have been awarded the kingly position, but his sin robbed him of the crown (Gen. 49:3–4; 35:22). Jacob gave the crown to Judah and the firstborn privileges to Joseph's sons, Ephraim and Manasseh. Simeon and Levi were so angry at the way Shechem treated their sister that they became murderers (Gen. 34). Jesus warned us against the destructive power of sinful anger (Matt. 5:21–26). When Joshua assigned each tribe its inheritance in Canaan, Simeon was absorbed into Judah and the Levitical priests were scattered into forty-eight towns in the other tribes (Josh. 21).

Jacob spoke to Judah and emphasized the faithfulness of God (Gen. 49:8–12). The kings of Israel from David to Zedekiah were descendants of

Judah, and when the nation divided, the southern kingdom, where David's descendants still reigned, was called the kingdom of Judah. The blessing Jacob gave to Judah certainly rested on David, for he defeated the enemies of the Jews and established a strong kingdom. Not all of David's successors were faithful to God, but the Lord was faithful to His people and kept David's lamp burning (1 Kings 15:4–5). This was important because the promised Redeemer would come from David's line (Isa. 11:10). Genesis 49:10 certainly points to our Lord Jesus Christ, the Lion of the tribe of Judah.

This leads us to the triumph of God's grace (Rev. 5). Jesus is both the Lion and the Lamb (Rev. 5:5–6), the Ruler and the Redeemer, the Sovereign and the Sacrifice. The Lamb died to cleanse us from sin, and the Lion lives and reigns to defeat our enemies. The Lamb points to the cross, while the Lion points to the crown. As we follow the news of the world, we sometimes wonder how long the Lord will allow wickedness to go on without being judged, and then we remember two facts: Christ the Lamb died for the sins of the world and offers sinners salvation, and Christ the Lion will one day roar and judge sinners justly (Acts 17:30–31).

Jacob said, "The King is coming" (see Gen. 49:10), and Pilate said to the Jewish mob, "Look, here is your king!" (John 19:14). Isaac asked his father, Abraham, "Where is the lamb?" (Gen. 22:7 NASB1995), and John the Baptist cried, "Behold, the Lamb of God" (John 1:29 NASB1995). God the Father in His grace sent Jesus the Lamb to be the Savior of the world (1 John 4:14). One day those who have not been cleansed by "the blood of the Lamb" (Rev. 7:14) will experience "the wrath of the Lamb" (Rev. 6:16). In these many ways and more, Jesus fulfills the promises to Abraham, Isaac, and Jacob. And He is your promised King too, if your faith is in Him.

1. Jesus said, "Salvation comes through the Jews" (John 4:22). Our Lord Jesus is a Jew of David's line. God chose to work through the nation of Israel. Consider the blessing it is to be called "the people of God" and how, in this age of the church, you and I share in this blessing!

2. Those who are "in Christ" have had their sins dealt with by Christ and are forgiven and free. Take a moment to thank God for His salvation today!

Moses: The Freeing Father

Read Exodus 3; Psalm 106:21–48

No matter how we measure him, Moses stands out in Scripture as a great leader. The Lord gave him the difficult assignment of transforming an entire nation from living for the Egyptians to living for the Lord, ready to claim their inheritance as the people of God. Our churches today need leaders who will stay with God's people long enough to move them toward maturity in the Lord (Heb. 5:11–14).

God prepares His leaders. As a child, Moses was raised in a godly home (Heb. 11:23) and then moved to Pharaoh's palace to learn "all the wisdom of the Egyptians" (Acts 7:22). But he needed to learn patience, for at age forty, he impulsively killed an Egyptian and had to flee. For the next forty years, he was a shepherd in Midian because the people he would be leading were just like sheep, even as we are (Num. 27:15–17; Ps. 100:3). God patiently prepared him for forty years of service, during which he delivered Israel from bondage and relocated them forty-two times (Num. 33) until they came to the gateway to the Promised Land.

We don't know our own potential, but God does. Two extremes we must avoid are overrating ourselves and underrating ourselves. "Don't think you are better than you really are. Be honest in your evaluation of yourselves, measuring yourselves by the faith God has given us" (Rom.

12:3). Forty years as a shepherd had mellowed Moses, and he felt God was making a mistake in calling him (Ex. 3:1—4:17). This was not a display of false humility, because Moses was sure he was a failure. But God knew better. It's wrong to brag about what we don't have, but it's also wrong to deny what God knows we do have. God's calling is God's enabling; we just humbly obey. "The LORD will work out his plans for my life" (Ps. 138:8).

Becoming new takes time. It's been said that it took only one night to take the Israelites out of Egypt but forty years to take Egypt out of the Israelites. Moses had to teach them the law at Mount Sinai so they knew how to worship God and how to get along with one another. How often they complained about both Moses and the Lord and desired to return to Egypt! And how often Moses had to intercede for the people and rescue them from judgment! Unbelief and complaining are marks of immaturity, and Moses had to wait for that old generation to die off before he could prepare the new generation for entering the Promised Land.

Transformers fight many battles. The people tired of the heavenly manna and wanted flesh to eat, and Moses was ready to give up (Num. 11:10–15). He was so irritated by the people that he struck the rock instead of speaking to it, and God had to discipline him (Num. 20:1–13). Some of the tribal leaders challenged his leadership (Num. 16), and even his own sister and brother criticized him (Num. 12). How patient both God and Moses were with the people!

Transformers must be faithful. Moses made mistakes, as we all do, and had his difficult days, but he was faithful to do his work to the glory of God (Num. 12:7; Heb. 3:1–5). Moses wasn't always popular or successful in the eyes of the people, but he was faithful to the Lord. "Now, a person who is put in charge as a manager must be faithful" (1 Cor. 4:2). He knew God, he prayed, he loved the people, he taught the Word, and he had faith in God.

1. Access a Bible dictionary, and look up the name for God in Exodus 3:14 (it might be listed as I AM, Jehovah, Yahweh, or YHWH). Study what this name means. The same God who spoke to Moses speaks to us!
2. Are you arguing with God about a step He wants you to take? Let Moses's example help you to say yes.

Day 19

Moses: Life Is a Journey

Read Hebrews 11:13–16, 24–29; 2 Corinthians 5:1–10

Since ancient days, authors and poets have used journeys and battles as metaphors for life itself. The Greek poet Homer wrote *The Iliad* about the Trojan War and *The Odyssey* about the ten-year journey of Odysseus as he returned home after the war. Biblical writers have used both images many times: the battle and the journey. Israel arrived at Kadesh-barnea about two years after their exodus from Egypt (the battle), but in their unbelief refused to enter the land (Num. 13–14). They spent the next thirty-eight years marching around in the wilderness until everybody twenty years of age and older had died, and then Joshua led them into the Promised Land (the journey). The book of Hebrews uses these events to encourage us to mature in our faith and claim our spiritual inheritance in Christ (Heb. 1–4). Since Christians are "temporary residents and foreigners" in this world (1 Pet. 2:11), let's consider Israel's journey and gain some encouragement from it.

The geography of the Bible is important. Egypt represents the bondage of this world, the condition of the lost sinner. Israel was delivered from death that first Passover by the blood of the lambs and from Egypt by the power of God when He opened the Red Sea. *The Lord didn't tell His people to stay in Egypt and help rebuild the country.* God wanted *separation*, not restoration. He had a great inheritance for them in Canaan, just as we have our spiritual inheritance in Christ. The Bible is both our road map and our bankbook. It marks out the path we should walk, and it tells us how rich we are in Christ.

The Lord has an appointed way for each of His children, and we must obey His will. If we do, we will not wander aimlessly, wasting time and energy, but be guided "along right paths, bringing honor to his name" (Ps. 23:3). God didn't lead Israel out of Egypt by the shortest way; shortcuts can be dangerous (Ex. 13:17–18). As long as we accept His will and obey it, He will always provide what we need and protect us from the Enemy. The way may not always be easy, but it will never be impossible. And though we may not understand all that the Father is doing, we know that He will never fail us.

The "slave mentality" of the people of Israel was what hindered them the most; they repeatedly asked to go back to Egypt. They wanted to return to the security they had as slaves, forgetting the price they were paying. Prisoners released from the penitentiary after many years of confinement sometimes commit further crimes so they can go back behind bars and have security. But God wanted Israel to leave their slavery behind and live righteous and free (Lev. 26:13). And He wants us who are of the family of faith today to likewise enjoy freedom and not go back into bondage (Gal. 5:1).

Life is a journey because we must make progress and mature in the faith. To stand still is eventually to go backward. We enter life through a narrow gate and walk on a narrow road (Matt. 7:13–14). We can't bring our sinful "baggage" with us, and we must not go on detours! The Lord says, "This is the way you should go" (Isa. 30:21), and we obey Him. Because life is a journey, its pace varies, its challenges change, its opportunities and problems come and go, but the Lord is always with us and we need never be afraid. One day this life of faith will end at the Father's house, where we shall dwell forever, having endured the battles and finished the journey.

1. Has there been a time in your life when God relocated you (physically or spiritually) to help you progress on life's journey?

2. How does it encourage you to take the long view of the journey, knowing the goal is heaven and the destiny is to be like Christ?

Moses: Matured by the Journey

Read Psalm 131; Lamentations 3:22–27; Ephesians 4:14–16

The very life in our bodies depends on change. As bad air is exhaled, cells are replaced and repaired, and without these and other changes, life and growth would end. As generations come and go, society itself has opportunities to change and be creative. We watch the gradual changing of the seasons and marvel at the natural world God created for us. Sudden change frightens us, while slow change is hardly noticed—especially in ourselves! Our bodies change and, if we're maturing as we should be, our minds and values change as well. We build character.

The people of Israel didn't want change. As they made their way from Egypt to Canaan, they frequently begged Moses to take them back to Egypt. They had been slaves for so long that even painful bondage with security was better than wearisome pilgrimage and insecurity. To them, it was better to be slaves living in houses than free people living in tents.

But their journey was teaching them about God and about themselves. Ralph Waldo Emerson quipped, "No change of circumstances can repair a defect of character."[1] He might have added that experiencing change is one of the best ways to discover our flaws. What life does to us depends largely on what life finds in us. After they crossed the Red Sea, the Israelites sang praises to the Lord, but it wasn't long before they were complaining (Ex. 15).

Both in the physical and the spiritual, God wants us to grow up and not just grow old (Heb. 5:11–14). Age is an accumulation of years, the automatic passing of time, while maturity is the evaluation and assimilation of experience that results in character, discernment, and self-control. Maturing people have "put away childish things" (1 Cor. 13:11) and are living by values, not prices. They don't expect to have their own way, nor are they constantly complaining and expecting instant attention. To be maturing in Christ means to understand and appreciate His present high priestly ministry in heaven and to go to the throne of grace and draw upon those heavenly resources for ourselves and others (Heb. 4:14–16).

In all the wilderness changes, as the people twenty years old and older died off, the Lord was preparing the new Israelite generation for life in their Promised Land. They were learning to listen and obey, to live together in community, to respect authority and be grateful for all the Lord did for them. Selfishness is usually a mark of childishness; sharing and gratitude are marks of the mature. As the Lord weans us away from infancy and moves us into maturity (Ps. 131), we must stop fretting and start submitting. The child must learn to live without mother's pampering, to evaluate opportunities, make decisions, and accept defeats.

"Jesus grew in wisdom and in stature and in favor with God and all the people" (Luke 2:52). He had balanced growth—intellectually, physically, spiritually, and socially—and He lived a balanced life as He served others. Isn't that what maturity is all about?

1. Israel frequently had a battle of wills with Moses and God. How do you see the maturing process producing cooperation?

2. The ability to self-identify areas of immaturity is a critical part of the journey to maturity. Reflect honestly on your life, and consider what transformation the Lord might want to make in you.

Day 21

Moses: Maturity Exercises Faith

Read Psalm 90; Luke 17:5–10

Life is much easier when we can stay at home, where things are familiar and tend to be safe. According to Numbers 33, the people of Israel changed locations forty-two times in their march from Egypt to Canaan, and their circumstances frequently irritated them. But if we have faith in our God, the changes He permits in our lives will build us up and not tear us down, and we will also be able to encourage others. In Psalm 90:1, Moses gives us the secret of his own peace of mind in the midst of those many changes: "Lord, through all the generations you have been our home!" *No matter how many times you may change your address, if the Lord is your home, you need not be upset.* This is the Old Testament version of Christ's words "abide in Me" (NASB1995) or "remain in me" (John 15:1–10). Situations change, but God says, "I am the LORD, and I do not change" (Mal. 3:6). Our spiritual home built by faith needs no reconstruction or relocation.

Faith is obeying God's Word in spite of the feelings within us, the circumstances around us, or the consequences before us. Israel's first address change was when Jacob's family moved to Egypt to be with Joseph. Old Jacob wanted to be sure he had God's approval for this move, and the Lord spoke to him one night and assured him he could go (Gen. 46:1–4). The basis of our faith is always the Word of God, because we live by promises and not by explanations. The nation expressed its faith even more when they obeyed the Passover instructions and put the lambs' blood on the lintels of their house doors.

It was during the march to Canaan that the changes came frequently and the nation had to exercise faith, but the Lord saw them through. We find it difficult to understand why they complained so much after seeing what God did in His judgment of Egypt, especially at the Red Sea when the Egyptian army was drowned. Certainly they should have seen clearly that the Lord was on their side and possessed the wisdom and power needed in each situation. But before we judge them, we need to examine our own lives and see how many times we have grumbled to ourselves, to others, and even to the Lord because of difficult circumstances.

It's dangerous to grow comfortable in the Christian life. Those who are in the process of becoming new know that comfort is but a short step from conforming to the world (Rom. 12:2). The bigger our comfort zone, the smaller will be our faith and the fewer our victories. If we hope to grow from *no faith* (Mark 4:40) to *little faith* (Matt. 14:31) to *great faith* (Matt. 8:10), we must stop complaining and let God have His way.

Three phrases from the Bible have helped me in this matter of restless complaining: "sit still" (Ruth 3:18 NKJV), "stand still" (Ex. 14:13), and "be still" (Ps. 46:10). Ruth could *sit still* because her beloved kinsman-redeemer was working for her, just as Jesus is interceding for us today. Israel could *stand still* because the Lord would open the way for His people and close the way for the enemy. All of us can *be still* because He is God and the Lord of Heaven's Armies!

"Show us how to increase our faith," the apostles said to Jesus, and He pointed to a mustard seed (Luke 17:5–6). It had life in it, and living faith grows as we follow the Lord. The end result of a maturing faith is faithfulness (Luke 17:7–10).

1. Reread Psalm 90:12–17 and meditate on the reasons Moses made these requests to God.
2. In what ways might God be asking you to step outside your comfort zone to walk with Him by faith?

Day 22

Moses: Faith Must Be Tested

Read Exodus 16:1–7; Deuteronomy 8:1–10

It's no coincidence that as God took His people out of the furnace of Egypt (Deut. 4:20) and into the Promised Land, the route He led them through was the dry wilderness of Sinai. In Egypt He heard their cries, and in the Promised Land He assured their abundance, but in the wilderness He ordained their testing. Such is often the way of faith. Between God's promises and provision is often pain. Following the Lord is easy when the battles are few and His victory assured. Trusting the Lord when we are in the wilderness and can't see the victory takes faith. And faith that cannot be tested cannot be trusted.

Jesus used the wilderness as a backdrop for testing faith in the parable of the seed and the soils (Matt. 13:3–9, 18–23). The shallow soil represents the hearts of people who have never repented, believed, or produced spiritual fruit, even though they expressed joy as they professed to receive Christ. The shoots came up, but there were no roots, and when you have no roots, you can produce no fruit. Sunshine is good for plants only if the plants are rooted and taking in water. New believers are tested by persecution so they can demonstrate whether they are truly born again.

Those who are true believers will experience further testing of their faith because they live in a world that does not know Christ (Matt. 5:11–12; John 15:18—16:4). Too many believers have the unbiblical notion that belonging to Christ and obeying Him guarantees the end of trouble, when actually trials are the mark of the faithful Christian (2 Tim. 3:12; 1 Pet. 4:12–19). Peter tells us to rejoice when people persecute us, because persecution is an honor. "The apostles left the high council rejoicing that God had counted them worthy to suffer disgrace for the name of Jesus" (Acts 5:41). Paul called this "the fellowship of His sufferings" (Phil. 3:10 NASB1995).

Suffering brings blessings in this life and also in the world to come. "God blesses those who patiently endure testing and temptation. Afterward they will receive the crown of life that God has promised to those who love him" (James 1:12). One of the main reasons the Lord allows our faith to be tested is for us to see His glory and no longer fall into temptation. The Lord had to satisfy the needs of His people in a place where they could not help themselves, and often God puts us in situations where we require more faith than is comfortable. In the wilderness our faith can be tested so that we may know that God can be trusted. Imagine the faith of the Israelites the day after Moses declared, "In the morning you will see the glory of the LORD" (Ex. 16:7).

Life is a journey God plans for us, and that journey involves changes, some of which we don't enjoy. Faith is what makes the difference. God tests our faith and gives us opportunities to glorify Christ in our witness, our work, and our walk. "So after you have suffered a little while, he will restore, support, and strengthen you, and he will place you on a firm foundation" (1 Pet. 5:10)—so don't give up! God gives strength for the journey and hope for the battle. He will reward your faith.

1. How have the tests of faith that you've endured brought you to trust God more fully?
2. Take a moment to reflect on James 1:12 and turn it into a prayer of thankfulness and faith.

Moses: Tested Faith Produces Character

Read Deuteronomy 8:11–18;
1 Corinthians 10:1–13; Hebrews 1:1–3

"Reputation is made in a moment, but character is built in a lifetime." I do not know who first said that, but it's inscribed on one of my coffee mugs. The statement marks the difference between the temporary "well-known people" and the permanent "great people." The word *character* comes from a Greek word that means "an engraving tool, to stamp as on a coin."[1] It is used only once in the original text of the New Testament in Hebrews 1:3: "The Son radiates God's own glory and expresses the very character of God." In other words, Jesus Christ is God because He possesses all the attributes of God (John 1:18; Phil. 2:6; Col. 1:15).

Dr. D. Martyn Lloyd-Jones said to me one day, "It's too bad when people succeed before they are ready for it." Talent is one thing; character is quite something else. Talent is what people see us do, but character is what God knows we are. God spent years building and testing the character of transformers like Joseph, Joshua, Hannah, David, Abigail, Jeremiah, Peter, and Paul, and that's why they accomplished God's will and ended well. Good character is the foundation for good conduct; each of us is both the sculptor and the marble. Fame may determine what we can receive from others, but character determines what we can give to others. Trials test us and build our endurance, and "endurance develops strength of character" (Rom. 5:3–4).

By the time the people of Israel arrived at the gateway to Canaan, the old generation was dead (except for Joshua and Caleb) and a new generation stood before Joshua, awaiting his orders. These were the people who remembered the Lord and obeyed His commands and passed the test. This new generation had grown up during forty years of trials and had passed the tests and developed faith and character. They were not perfect, and neither was Joshua, but they had the vision of victors and the character of conquerors. They followed God's orders and claimed their inheritance by faith, because true faith and true character go together.

The immature person skips class when the tests are given and invariably asks, "What is safe and easy?" but the person of character asks, "What is right? What will honor God?" Life is built on character, and character is built on decisions. We sometimes forget our decisions, but our decisions never forget us. Above all, we must never forget our God (Deut. 8:11). If we fail the test, we must remember that God will forgive sin and mend character if we humbly ask Him, but we must be honest and sincere. He restored Abraham after he fled to Egypt (Gen. 12), David after he committed adultery and had the husband killed (2 Sam. 11–12), and Peter after he denied the Lord (John 21). "LORD, if you kept a record of our sins, who, O Lord, could ever survive? But you offer forgiveness, that we might learn to fear you" (Ps. 130:3–4). True repentance requires remembering the faithfulness of God and leads to a greater fear of the Lord.

We ought never to despise the trials in life that the Lord allows to refine us and shape us. Before the Israelites could experience the blessings of their inheritance in the Promised Land, they had to endure the testing of their faith. The same is true of us today. Peter puts it most eloquently when he writes to the persecuted believers, "There is wonderful joy ahead, even though you must endure many trials for a little while. These trials will show that your faith is genuine. It is being tested as fire tests and purifies gold—though your faith is far more precious than mere gold. So when your faith remains strong through many trials, it will bring you much praise and glory and honor on the day when Jesus Christ is revealed to the whole world" (1 Pet. 1:6–7).

1. Drawing on today's Scriptures and reading, how would you define "godly character"?
2. First Corinthians 10:1–13 teaches us to learn from the mistakes of others. If we don't, we learn the hard way. What is your learning style?

Day 24

Moses: Character Brings Freedom

Read Deuteronomy 11; John 8:31–38

One of my favorite collections of comics is *Calvin and Hobbes*. Whenever Calvin has to endure eating vegetables or doing yard work, his father constantly shrugs off his protests and repeats that it "builds character."[1] Character building is one of the main goals of family life. Parents protect and train children to become mature so they can grow up and be equipped in mind and body to take their place in the adult world. Children who lack character often lose privileges. But children who have matured and passed some tests in the home often are rewarded with more freedom and opportunities. Ideally, mature children leave the home and flourish on their own because they know how to accept responsibility.

In the wilderness, God was teaching His children how to handle their freedom in the new land. Freedom does not mean the privilege of doing anything we want to do. *Freedom is life controlled by truth and motivated by love, all to the glory of God.* For the Israelites, the testing in the wilderness proved their character and trust in the Lord, and for that reason God blessed them with freedom. How were they to use this new freedom? Not for themselves but for the glory of God!

This is one of life's fundamental paradoxes: freedom requires submission. In the words of P. T. Forsyth, "The first duty of every soul is to find not its freedom but its Master." When the gifted musician submits to the authority of a master conductor, or the gifted athlete to a great coach, both find the freedom to release their abilities and achieve greatness. Forsyth concludes, "Liberty in itself is not an end; and it has only the worth of its end."[2]

What is the end of the Christian life? This is essentially the same question the lawyer asked Jesus: "Which is the greatest commandment?" The greatest commandment is twofold: to know and love the one and only God and, accordingly, to love your neighbor as yourself (Mark 12:28–31). The goal of freedom in the Christian life is to develop ourselves fully so we can obey God and serve others for His glory. Freedom we use only for ourselves is bondage. Focusing only on ourselves and being indifferent toward others is actually worse than declaring war on others. But bondage to Jesus Christ brings joyful freedom to us and to others as God works in and through us.

Free people are motivated by love, not by selfishness, prejudice, hatred, or gain. "Love is patient and kind. Love is not jealous or boastful or proud or rude. It does not demand its own way. It is not irritable, and it keeps no record of being wronged" (1 Cor. 13:4–5). If our faith has been tested by fire, our character will give us this outward-looking love for God and neighbor that is not easily offended and seeks the good in others. Faith that has failed in the fire will continue to ask "What's in it for me?"

We must take seriously Jesus's words: "If the Son sets you free, you are truly free" (John 8:36). In the wilderness, Moses was on the front lines of liberation with Pharaoh, but it was God who loosed the chains. Likewise, we cannot create our own freedom apart from God. It's only by the Son, Jesus Christ, who by His death and resurrection broke the chains of sin for us, redeemed us from our slavery to iniquity, and set us free to follow Him as our Master. We are free to live by the truth, motivated by love, for the glory of God.

1. God often offers us a choice that leads to blessings. Did you notice all the "if" statements in Deuteronomy 11 that include God's promises to bless? If not, go back and read those again.

2. Tested faith produces character, which yields freedom. Is your version of freedom dependent on anyone other than God?

Day 25

Moses: The Farewell Speech

Read Deuteronomy 6:1–9;
11:1, 18–25; 34:1–12

In reality, the entire book of Deuteronomy is Moses's farewell speech to the new generation of Israelites who were about to enter the Promised Land. *Deuteronomy* means "second law." In it, Moses was rehearsing the law given in Exodus and applying it to the Israelites' lives in their new land. Moses emphasized two words in Deuteronomy: *remember* and *love*. The Israelites were to remember what God had done for them and their ancestors, and they were to love the Lord and obey Him and not get tangled up with the idols of the people in the land. Romans 13:8–13 makes it clear that love for the Lord should be the greatest motivation for our obedience.

Moses had seen many new beginnings during the forty years he led the nation, starting with the changes in his own life. The Lord had transformed him from a fugitive into a powerful leader who prepared Joshua and the people for the conquest of Canaan. In Egypt, Moses and the people had seen water transformed into blood and day transformed into the darkest night. They saw God transform the water of the Red Sea into walls and the seabed into a solid, dry highway for them to walk on. "He made a dry path through the Red Sea, and his people went across on foot" (Ps. 66:6).

One of the neglected transformations in the wilderness march involves the covetous prophet Balaam, whom King Balak hired to curse the Israelites (Num. 22–24). "But the LORD your God refused to listen to Balaam. He turned the intended curse into a blessing because the LORD your God loves you" (Deut. 23:5). Nehemiah used this text as the springboard for his reformation of the unlawful marriages of the Israelites to pagan women (Neh. 13:1–3).

When the hireling prophet tried to curse Israel, he ended up blessing them instead! Often in Bible history and church history, God has transformed the enemy's curses and attacks into God's blessings. Think of Joseph's experiences in Egypt, Paul's thorn in the flesh (2 Cor. 12:1–10), and the death of Jesus on the cross. At the same time, let's remember that our own willful disobedience can transform God's blessings into curses (Mal. 2:1–2).

Moses's greatest disappointment was God prohibiting his entry into the Promised Land (Num. 20:1–13), but even that disappointment was transformed! Moses finally made it to the Holy Land when he and Elijah joined Jesus in His glory on the Mount of Transfiguration (Matt. 17:1–8). They talked with Jesus about the "exodus" He would accomplish at Jerusalem (Luke 9:30). His death on the cross would set sinners free from sin, just as the blood of the lamb set Israel free from death in Egypt, and He would ascend to heaven as Elijah did. One of the joys of heaven will be learning how God turned curses into blessings when we were serving on earth.

God could transform curses into blessing, *but He could not change the people's hearts without their cooperation.* That entire generation rebelled so often that God just let them die off, and He started afresh with the new generation. Jesus had a similar experience with the people of Israel who would not receive Him (Luke 13:34). Let us, instead, give God permission to transform all of who we are!

1. Moses lived what he declared in his farewell speech. We seldom get the chance to deliver our farewell before we die. What would you say to your family if you had the chance?
2. God changes hearts insofar as we are willing to cooperate with Him. Ask God to give you a heart that trusts and obeys Him.

Day 26

Joshua: The Successor

Read Deuteronomy 31:7–8; Joshua 1:5; 21:45; 23:14

The Lord appointed Joshua to succeed Moses, and the choice was a good one. Joshua had known both hardship in Egypt and trials in the wilderness, and he was an experienced general who had led Israel's army to victory during their journey. God made it clear that the key to Israel's conquest of Canaan was faith in God and obedience to His Word (Deut. 31:7–8; Josh. 1:6–9). Although leaders must deal with failure, twice Joshua reminded the nation that not one word of God's promises had failed (Josh. 21:45; 23:14).

Numbers can fail. When Israel arrived at Kadesh-barnea, about two years after their exodus from Egypt, they sent twelve men into Canaan to spy out the land. Joshua and Caleb were the only spies who were confident that God could and would give them victory. The rest had no faith and wanted to return to Egypt (Num. 13–14). God's response was to slay the ten unbelieving spies and over the next thirty-eight years allow the unbelieving older generation to die. The ten spies and the people twenty years old and older were living by sight and not by faith. You would think that among the millions of people in the nation, more would have shown faith, but they did not. They all failed to trust the Lord.

Experts can fail. Joshua had excellent soldiers, but soldiers are people and subject to temptation to sin. The army conquered Jericho but failed at Ai because there was sin in the camp (Josh. 6–7). The people were warned not to take any of the spoils from Jericho, but Achan had stolen a beautiful robe and some silver and gold, and this displeased the Lord. Note that it was Israel that was guilty, not just Achan alone (7:1, 11). Ananias and Sapphira in Acts 5 show us that even church members can rob God and hurt the church. Indeed, the sins of one can affect and infect others and bring guilt on the whole body (Gal. 5:9). Even still, Joshua was able to use the army's "loss" to deceive the people of Ai and finally defeat them.

Gifted leaders can fail. Joshua seems to have been somewhat impetuous. He didn't seek God's will about attacking Ai; otherwise, he would have known about Achan's sin. In Joshua 9:14, the Gibeonites deceived Joshua and his leaders who "did not consult the LORD." This meant not only that Israel could not destroy the Gibeonites but also that Israel had to defend them, and that's what happened (Josh. 10). Had the leaders been cautious and sought guidance from the Lord, they would have avoided this embarrassing situation and defeated an enemy. "Only simpletons believe everything they're told! The prudent carefully consider their steps" (Prov. 14:15).

God never fails! Perhaps this is the greatest characteristic of God to consider here: He is faithful. He is always true to His people, His Word, and His promises. If we need wisdom, He supplies it (James 1:5). If we need victory, His Word tells us, "For every child of God defeats this evil world, and we achieve this victory through our faith" (1 John 5:4). "For all of God's promises have been fulfilled in Christ with a resounding 'Yes!' And through Christ, our 'Amen' (which means 'Yes') ascends to God for his glory" (2 Cor. 1:20).

1. In Deuteronomy 31:7–8, Moses speaks to Joshua for God. In Joshua 1:5, God Himself speaks to Joshua. What is the heart of the promises made to Joshua in those verses?
2. How did Joshua rise above the failures to be a successful leader?

Day 27

Samson: The Defiled and Defeated

Read Judges 14

Samson is remembered as much for his weaknesses as for his great strength, and one of his weaknesses was women. His God-given task was to begin to deliver Israel from the Philistines (Judg. 13:5), so why did he decide to marry a Philistine woman? His best man ended up marrying her, and God used this event to incite Samson to attack the enemy (Judg. 14:19–20; 15:1–5), but Samson was still disobedient. On his way to Timnah with his parents, he was attacked by a lion, which he killed with his bare hands, throwing the body to the side of the road. Later, on his way to the wedding, he turned from the path to see if the lion's carcass was still there. As a Nazirite, Samson was not permitted to touch a dead body, so why was he interested in the remains of the lion? (Judg. 14:5–9; Num. 6.) Was this an act of pride? Was he basking in the glory of his victory instead of giving the glory to the Lord?

When he ate the honey from the lion's carcass, he defiled himself and ceased to be a dedicated Nazirite. "But the young man needed something to eat," someone might argue, forgetting that a Nazirite's first obligation is to please the Lord and not his own appetite. Honey would give him energy, but defilement would take away his dedication to the Lord. Samson still had his strength and was able to attack the enemy, but he lost the approval and blessing of God. Not only did he sin, but he also jested about the lion and turned his sin into a riddle (Judg. 14:12–18). To sin is one thing, but to joke about the sin is to make things worse.

A university student complained to me that she had to read a book that was anything but sanctifying, and I suggested she ask the professor for permission to read a different book and recommended a title. He gave her permission, and I loaned her a copy of the book. I don't doubt that there are some good things in the first book, but why dig honey out of a rotten carcass? Delight that leads to defilement also could lead to defeat.

There is a delight found in opening the Bible and tasting the goodness of God. "How sweet your words taste to me; they are sweeter than honey" (Ps. 119:103; see also 19:10). The world's "sweetness" is usually mixed with "a craving for physical pleasure, a craving for everything we see, and pride in our achievements and possessions" (1 John 2:16). We ought rather to be like the prophet Jeremiah, who let the Word of God come into his heart as if he had devoured it like a meal (Jer. 15:16).

American author Ernest Hemingway once wrote, "What is moral is what you feel good after and what is immoral is what you feel bad after."[1] But how foolish it is to determine right and wrong after the fact—and based upon feelings! I have had several operations and usually felt miserable after them, but they were all good for me nonetheless. No doubt Samson felt good after eating the honey, but from that time on he was a defiled ex-Nazirite on a downhill detour. Delilah stole his strength and then handed him over to the Philistines, who made a public spectacle of him. He ended his career by pulling down a heathen temple and killing himself and thousands of Philistines (Judg. 16). It was a courageous feat, but God had a better plan, and Samson missed it.

1. Why do you think Samson made all those mistakes?
2. Is there any area in your life in which you are tempted to bring honey out of a rotten carcass?

Ruth: The Dutiful

Read Ruth 1–4

One of missionary Amy Carmichael's poems begins with a phrase that has arrested my attention: "the quiet joy of duty."[1] Not everybody identifies duty with quietness and joy; too often, duty is associated with grumbling and misery. The child asks, "Do I have to?" The employee says, "Why is it always me?" The frustrated parent says, "What, must I again?" Yet this phrase, "the quiet joy of duty," is an apt description of Ruth, the great-grandmother of King David and one of the most attractive and godly women in Bible history.

When you read the story of Ruth, you meet a woman who worked hard and never complained and whose character and conduct were so exemplary that Boaz, one of the wealthiest men in Bethlehem, wanted to marry her, and he did! Ruth was a new convert, won to faith in the Lord by the love and concern of her mother-in-law, Naomi. Both of them were widows and could have been angry with the Lord, but they loved the Lord and each other and served each other in a beautiful way.

Gleaning in the harvest field, Ruth stood out from the rest of the workers. Boaz noticed her and gave her special privileges. She was humble and grateful, and he was smitten and generous. If Ruth had been campaigning for a husband, things might not have turned out that way, but because she was serving the Lord and caring for Naomi, the Lord providentially worked everything out. Ruth shows us what Jesus meant when He said, "Seek the Kingdom of God above all else, and live righteously, and he will give you everything you need" (Matt. 6:33). Duty is not a burden; it's an opportunity to receive blessing and be a blessing. Duty is service motivated by love, compelled by concern for others.

But duty is something else. Novelist Pearl Buck called duty "the other side of rights."[2] If I have the right to earn a living, then I also have the duty to do my best and be grateful for the job. If children have the privilege of being cared for by loving, sacrificing parents, they also have the duty to honor and obey them. We enjoy our rights, so we ought to enjoy "paying duty" in return. We are not serving "earthly masters" but the Lord Jesus Christ. Nor are we "doing a job" but doing the will of God—and we should do God's will from the heart (Eph. 6:5–8).

Ruth's commitment to her duty enabled her to be an agent of change and transformation. She turned Naomi's bitterness into joy (Ruth 1:20–21; 2:19–23), awakened love in Boaz, excited the city, and eventually gave Israel their greatest king, King David. In turn, David gave us many of the Psalms and also gave the world the King of Kings, our Lord Jesus Christ! We may not have those same privileges, but what we do will indeed glorify God and accomplish His will. Jesus said, "We must quickly carry out the tasks assigned us by the one who sent us. The night is coming, and then no one can work" (John 9:4). Each and every day presents us with opportunities to grow in the quiet joy of duty.

> 1. At the start of Ruth's story, Naomi was a "prickly" person and even called herself "bitter." But Ruth's dutiful service to her mother-in-law helped Naomi become "pleasant" again. Whom can you encourage by consistent, dutiful service?

2. Ruth was a widow and an immigrant when she arrived in Bethlehem. By story's end, Ruth was welcomed into the heart of the community. Whom can you take down barriers for and help to belong?

Day 29

Ruth: Quietness in Duty

Read Ruth 1:16–22; Isaiah 32:16–20; Philippians 4:6–9

Some jobs are very noisy, like the construction site or the pediatrician's office, but lack of noise isn't what "the quiet joy of duty" is referring to. It's telling us that the work or the workplace may be noisy and confusing but the heart of the worker is quietly content. It's what Peter called "the unfading beauty of a gentle and quiet spirit" (1 Pet. 3:4). During His three busy years of ministry, our Lord was under constant pressure, particularly as He drew near to the cross. Yet He was always at peace and in control of things, performing each duty with quiet joy.

After her confession of faith in 1:16–17, Ruth says very little in the rest of the book, but her actions speak of calmness and purpose. Once she learned from Naomi that Boaz was their kinsman, she knew that all was well. "Just be patient, my daughter," Naomi told her. "The man won't rest until he has settled things today" (3:18). And she was right. Ruth was able to rest and quiet her anxiety, knowing the Lord was working things for her good.

In a world filled with noise and distraction, what is the secret of a quiet heart? Paul explains it in Philippians 4:6–9: Pray with thanksgiving about everything (v. 6), meditate only on that which is true and good (v. 8), and do what God tells you to do (v. 9). If we follow this counsel, the peace of God will guard us (v. 7) and the God of peace be with us (v. 9). Our Lord's command to us is, "Don't let your hearts be troubled" (John 14:1). As we read the Word, meditate, and pray, it's our responsibility to focus on the Lord and claim His promises. When we find ourselves thinking about that which is out of bounds for believers, we must abandon it and trust Christ for His peace.

Isaiah tells us that righteousness and justice bring peace, so we must be right with God and others if we expect to have a quiet heart. We must be at peace with God (Rom. 5:1) before we can enjoy the peace of God. Unconfessed sins, unfulfilled promises, unfinished work, and unsettled disagreements with others will all rob us of the quietness and confidence the Father wants us to enjoy day by day. A cleansed heart and conscience are essential for a quiet heart that can face life with confidence.

Ruth and Naomi were poor, but Boaz was rich, and he arranged to share his riches with them in a beautiful and loving way: he married Ruth! In chapter 2, Ruth was living on the leftovers dropped in the field, and in chapter 3, she accepted the generous gift of Boaz. But when she became his wife, *all his wealth was available to her for the asking!* As God's children, we are united with Christ and blessed with "every spiritual blessing," the riches of his "kindness and grace," and "the endless treasures available ... in Christ" (Eph. 1:3, 7; 3:8). In this way, Ruth's story foreshadows the life of Jesus. He took upon Himself flesh and blood so that He might be our kinsman-redeemer and save us from our poverty and bondage (Heb. 2:14–15). We were too poor to buy our freedom, but He became poor to make us rich (2 Cor. 8:9).

The turning point came when Ruth put herself at the feet of her kinsman-redeemer and trusted him to do right. Mary, the sister of Martha, did the same (Luke 10:38–42). And when you find the quiet joy of following Christ, you become new too!

1. When we meet Naomi, she's blaming God for her suffering and emptiness (Ruth 1:13, 21). Is there an issue between you and God that needs to be settled so there can be peace?

2. Naomi and Ruth returned to Bethlehem as poor women. They took the next step: Ruth gathered the grain that was dropped by the reapers. What is the next simple step for you to become new?

Day 30

Ruth: Joy in Duty

Read Ruth 4:13–17; John 15:9–17; 17:13

The words *happiness* and *joy* are frequently used interchangeably, but I've tried to keep them separated in my own mind. The word *happy* comes from the Old Norse word *happ,* which means "luck, fortune."[1] Therefore, happiness depends on happenings, but joy is much deeper. True joy is a fruit of the Spirit (Gal. 5:22) and comes from a heart yielded to the Lord and trusting wholly in Him. Joy doesn't depend on circumstances or what people call "good luck." We can be joyful in the midst of bad happenings, like Paul and Silas in prison (Acts 16:25) or Jesus as He faced Calvary (John 17:13; Heb. 12:2). I have personally experienced inexplicably deep joy while being taken to the hospital in an ambulance after an auto accident caused by a drunken driver going eighty miles an hour. The joy was still there in the intensive care unit when they started attaching various devices to my wounded body.

The story of Ruth opens with its own accident of sorts, which produced sorrow upon sorrow: a severe famine, a family leaving home, three funerals, a lonely trip back home, poverty, and toil. But it ends with rejoicing: two widows redeemed from poverty, one widow married to a wealthy man, God sending the couple a baby son whose grandson David became Israel's greatest king. God doesn't always prevent sorrow, nor is sorrow always caused by sin. Grief is a natural response to physical and emotional pain and loss. But the Lord can give us joy *in the midst of pain and sorrow.*

"To pursue joy is to lose it," said Alexander Maclaren. "The only way to get it is to follow steadily the path of duty, without thinking of joy, and then ... it comes most surely unsought."[2] Joy is the by-product of faithfulness on the path of duty, accomplishing what the Lord wants us to do and has helped us to do. Even while we are doing our work, there is a quiet joy that moves us along. "Don't be dejected and sad, for the joy of the LORD is your strength" (Neh. 8:10). Joy rooted in God will sustain us in times of sadness and darkness. "Weeping may last through the night, but joy comes with the morning" (Ps. 30:5). If we walk by faith, our tears become seeds that produce a crop of joy. "Those who plant in tears will harvest with shouts of joy" (Ps. 126:5).

A truism in the church world is the acronym *J-O-Y*: Jesus, others, yourself. If we truly put Jesus first, others next, and ourselves last, our priorities are right and our hearts will be joyful. I hope the Lord can say of us what Paul said of Timothy: "I have no one else like Timothy, who genuinely cares about your welfare. All the others care only for themselves and not for what matters to Jesus Christ" (Phil. 2:20–21).

"Duty does not have to be dull," wrote Thomas Merton. "Love can make it beautiful and fill it with life."[3] Love for Jesus and love for others transforms us as we serve, and our service can help to transform others. Ruth and Naomi loved each other, and both of them loved the Lord God of Israel. Boaz loved Ruth and obeyed God's will in marrying her.

After our Lord taught the disciples about the vine and branches (John 15:1–8), He emphasized the experience of joy: "I have told you these things so that you will be filled with my joy. Yes, your joy will overflow!" (v. 11). Notice that first we are filled with Christ's joy; then our own joy overflows. Joyful Christians have hearts that know the joy of the Lord (17:13).

1. How do you differentiate between being "happy" and "joyful"?
2. Rather than asking yourself "Am I happy?" reflect on the question "Am I useful?"

Day 31

Hannah: The Gracious

Read 1 Samuel 1:1—2:11

The story of Ruth leads us into the story of Hannah, which is not remarkable because both women suffered greatly, submitted humbly to God's will, and gave birth to sons who played important roles in the history of Israel—King David and the prophet Samuel. Some people today see children as nuisances to be removed and not treasures to be protected, but Hannah wanted a son badly, and God graciously answered her prayers. The name Hannah means "grace" or "woman of grace," and in her humility, she embodied the truth that God "gives grace generously" (James 4:6).

Grace enables us to endure patiently. To be with a scathing critic who acts as our superior is one of life's greatest trials. Hannah was Elkanah's first wife, and he loved her dearly, but when she proved barren, he married a second time so that he might have a family to carry on his name. God doesn't always change or remove our enemies, but He does give us the grace we need to listen to spiteful words and not retaliate. Grace can turn pain into joyful maturity.

Grace enables us to trust God for help. Our God is "the God of all grace" (1 Pet. 5:10 NKJV), and His assurance is, "My grace is all you need" (2 Cor. 12:9). His throne is "the throne of grace" (Heb. 4:16 NKJV) and is always available to us. Perhaps Hannah remembered that Rachel, Jacob's favorite wife, once bore the same burden and that the Lord eventually gave her Joseph, a truly great son (Gen. 30:1–2, 22–24). Just about the time we say, "I can't stand this much longer," the Lord gives us the endurance we need. Endurance is essential for spiritual growth, for without it we can never learn anything. "So let it grow, for when your endurance is fully developed, you will be perfect and complete, needing nothing" (James 1:4).

Grace enables us to make sacrifices. The Lord gave Elkanah and Hannah a son whom she named Samuel, which means "asked of God." According to God's law, her husband could have canceled her vow, and the fact that he did not shows that he was in agreement with it (Num. 30:10–15). Their prayer was that Samuel would grow up to be a mighty servant of God, and it was answered. Israel's spiritual life was very low, and there was a desperate need for a leader to bring them back to the Lord. Like Isaac, Samuel was a "living sacrifice" given to the Lord (Gen. 22; Rom. 12:1). When God presents us with gifts, we should give them back to Him lest the gifts take the place of the Giver, which is idolatry.

Grace enables us to worship and praise God. Hannah took none of the credit for the birth of her son because Samuel was God's blessing. "Children are a gift from the LORD; they are a reward from him" (Ps. 127:3). A child is a gift to be loved and guarded, not a piece of garbage to be thrown away. "He gives the childless woman a family, making her a happy mother" (Ps. 113:9). Hannah's song of praise glorifies the Lord and magnifies His grace (1 Sam. 2:4–8). In fact, Hannah's example and experience must have had a profound impact on the Virgin Mary! (Luke 1:46–55).

Because God gave grace to Hannah to bear Samuel and grace to Mary to bear Jesus and because they each gave their sons to do the will of God, we are the ones who are blessed!

> 1. Do you have a constant critic in your life? How are you seeking grace to help?

2. In what ways could you minister to women burdened by infertility?

3. If you are a parent, have you dedicated your children to God? How do you pray for them?

Samuel: The Disappointed

Read 1 Samuel 8 and 12

A judge, a prophet, a priest, and a man of prayer, Samuel was appointed by God to serve during a difficult transition time in Israel's history. Eli the high priest taught him the law, but it was from his mother, Hannah, that he learned how to listen and obey and, most of all, how to pray. As a spiritual leader, Samuel is associated with Moses and Aaron (Ps. 99:6; Jer. 15:1) as well as Gideon and David (Heb. 11:32). During his long life, Samuel frequently met with disappointment as the leaders of the nation made unwise decisions and turned from following the Lord.

He was disappointed with the priests. Surely Samuel was disappointed with Eli and his sons (1 Sam. 2:12–36). Eli was Samuel's mentor, but Eli's sons were wicked men who used their priestly authority to please themselves. Their father scolded them mildly but never really disciplined them. Unfortunately, Samuel dealt with his sons the same way (1 Sam. 8:1–5). During his growing-up years, Samuel was kept pure by the Lord in the midst of hypocrisy, disobedience, and overt sin.

He was disappointed with nominal faith. Samuel was also disappointed in the so-called revival described in 1 Samuel 7, because it didn't deeply touch the hearts of the people. They had abandoned their idols, confessed their sins, and prayed, but then they "fired" Samuel and asked for a king when the Lord was their true King (1 Sam. 8). The elders wanted Israel to be like the Gentiles, forgetting that they were a special nation, chosen by the Lord to be set apart as a people (Num. 23:9–10; Ex. 19:1–6; 33:16). God told Samuel to give them a king because one of God's harshest disciplines is to let His people have their own way and suffer the consequences.

He was disappointed with the king. At first, Samuel was impressed with Saul, but then he became deeply disappointed as Saul disobeyed God's will and lied about it. Saul was more concerned with his reputation than his character, such that when David came on the scene, the king saw him as a dangerous rival and tried to kill him. Samuel had anointed David as king, and he and David secretly met together at the risk of their lives (1 Sam. 19:18–24). "Samuel never went to meet with Saul again, but he mourned constantly for him" (1 Sam. 15:35).

But Samuel did not abandon his ministry even though the leaders had abandoned him. In his farewell address, Samuel said, "As for me, I will certainly not sin against the LORD by ending my prayers for you. And I will continue to teach you what is good and right" (1 Sam. 12:23). He majored on the Word of God and prayer (Acts 6:4), and he ministered at what became known as the schools of the prophets and trained young men to serve God (1 Sam. 19:18–23). He also continued to visit the towns to help the people understand and obey the law (1 Sam 7:15–17).

When we experience disappointments, we must submit to God's appointments and obey Him. Our hearts may be broken, and we may grieve over "what might have been," but we must remember that when the Lord is not permitted to rule, He will overrule and accomplish His purposes. Our task is to obey Him and leave the consequences to Him. Praying "May Your will be done" can heal a despondent heart (Matt. 6:10) and eventually make things right. After all, there is a David waiting to ascend the throne!

1. The spiritual leaders of your church always need prayer, so ask God to help them know His will. Pray for the congregation, that they would respond rightly to God's will and to His appointed leaders.

2. Samuel anointed David to be king, so he knew God had a plan. Encourage yourself with this truth: The way things are now is not how they will stay, by God's grace.

Day 33

Saul: The Substitute

Read 1 Samuel 8; 13:1–14

The first king of Israel was Saul, the son of Kish. He was what we today would call a "control freak." He used people and abused people because he had to have his way in everything. If you questioned him, you were humiliated, and if you opposed him, you were eliminated.

Becoming new might result in one of two paths: changing from worse to better or changing from better to worse. Leaders often promise change, but they don't always tell us which kind to expect. Saul's own son Jonathan said, "My father has made trouble for us all" (1 Sam. 14:29). But Israel insisted on having a king "like all the other nations" (1 Sam. 8:5), and they paid for it dearly. When God's people abandon their spiritual distinctions and start imitating the world, they are heading for trouble.

Saul lived on substitutes. He substituted height for stature, and even Samuel was impressed by his physique (1 Sam. 10:23–24), a mistake Samuel made twice (1 Sam. 16:6–7). Because Saul did not have the moral and spiritual stature needed to command the people, he substituted dictatorship for leadership and ruled by force and fear, not by encouragement and example. He substituted excuses for reasons and always had an alibi when caught disobeying God (1 Sam. 13:11–12).

A "control freak" is ruthless when dealing with people, because people are only a means to an end. Saul offered one of his daughters as a wife to the man who killed Goliath (1 Sam. 17:25). If the soldiers hadn't intervened, Saul would have killed Jonathan for violating the king's foolish oath and eating some honey (1 Sam. 14:24–46). In his fear of losing control, Saul suspected anyone who didn't inflate his ego or who seemed to side with David, and he slaughtered eighty-five priests and their families because they helped David escape (1 Sam. 22:11–23). Saul is described perfectly in Ezekiel 34:1–10. He was not a true shepherd, for shepherds don't drive the sheep; they lead them and love them.

Yet Saul put on a "religious front" before the people. Instead of waiting for Samuel, Saul built an altar and offered sacrifices (1 Sam. 13:5–14). He boasted that he had obeyed the Lord when actually he had disobeyed, and then he begged Samuel to honor him before the people (1 Sam. 15:13, 30–31). Saul had no heart for God; his reputation trumped his character. Therefore, the Lord abandoned him (1 Sam. 16:14) and sent Samuel to anoint David (1 Sam. 16:1–13).

"I have been a fool and very, very wrong," Saul told David (1 Sam. 26:21), but it was an admission to man and not a confession to God. Instead of turning to the Lord, he sought out a medium (1 Sam. 28). Saul went into his final battle without God's blessing, was wounded, and committed suicide (1 Sam. 31). The king who stood so tall fell to the earth, and David later sang a funeral dirge with the refrain, "Oh, how the mighty heroes have fallen!" (2 Sam. 1:19, 25, 27).

Because Saul lived on substitutes, he became a substitute king. We learn from Saul the basic principle of life, that God wills to work in you before He works through you. Without an internal transformation, any external transformation we seek to impose will be revealed for what it is: a poor substitute for the real thing.

1. Under what circumstances was Saul's actual character revealed? How does this affirm the importance of God transforming us inwardly?

2. Ask God to shape your life in such a way that you become new for His glory!

Day 34

David: The Servant

Read 1 Samuel 16; Psalm 78:56–72

After the turbulent years of Saul's reign, how refreshing it was for Israel to have David on the throne, "a man after [God's] own heart" (1 Sam. 13:14). Saul had driven the people as once he had driven his father's donkeys, but David led his people as he had led his father's sheep. Saul stood over the people, but David stood by his people and fought their battles and won. Saul demanded his way, but David sought God's way. While his name literally means "beloved," more than thirty times in the Bible David's name is associated with the word *servant* (e.g., Pss. 78:70; 89:3, 20). The servant's heart will be seen in daily life. Notice the ways that Scripture reveals David's heart.

David served his family. David's early years were not spent idle but hard at work serving his father and brothers as a shepherd. When his father told him to take a food package to his brothers in Saul's army, David obeyed and ended up killing a giant (1 Sam. 17). *When God wants to provide successful leaders for His people, He begins with men and women who know how to serve.* Why? Because nobody has the right to exercise authority who has not first submitted to authority and obeyed (Matt. 25:21, 23). "First a servant, then a ruler" is God's approach. Even our Lord

Jesus Christ became a servant before He was exalted to the throne (Phil. 2:1–11; Luke 22:27).

David served King Saul. Despite Saul harboring bitterness and jealousy against him, David honored and served the king. When Saul experienced one of his "fits," David soothed him by playing the harp (1 Sam. 16:14–23). When Saul made David an officer in the army, hoping he would be killed in battle, God protected him and gave him great victories. "Whatever Saul asked David to do, David did it successfully" (1 Sam. 18:5). He became the most popular man in the army, and this made Saul more envious and dangerous. Saul even neglected his royal duties that he might concentrate on pursuing David, and David fled the court and moved about in the wilderness with his own small army. He never attacked Saul, though twice he could have killed him, and he never spoke evil of Saul.

David served the nation. When he became king, David served the nation faithfully, fighting their battles, expanding their borders, solving their problems, and encouraging their faith in the Lord. "He cared for them with a true heart and led them with skillful hands" (Ps. 78:72). He was a rare combination of soldier, poet, musician, and administrator, and God blessed and used these gifts.

David served the Lord. "My servant David" was not just a title; it was a living reality. We have every reason to believe that David obeyed Deuteronomy 17:18–20 as he honored God's Word. It was his heart's desire to build a temple for the Lord, but God had chosen David's son Solomon for that privilege, so David began to gather the wealth needed for that important project. He risked his life on the battlefield and collected the spoils for the treasury (1 Chron. 29:1–5). He organized the civil and military divisions of the land and also the ministry of the priests and Levites. He wrote worship hymns for the choirs and made musical instruments. Because David served the Lord, everything was in order and there was money in the bank when Solomon became king.

At the end of his days, David had served the Lord, his family, and his nation well. Certainly he heard, "Well done, good and faithful servant."

1. Read again the passages for today, and spot the "leadership principles" from above.
2. What part of David's service do you find true in your life?

Day 35

David: The Sufferer

Read Psalm 18

For all his virtues and victories, David was no stranger to suffering. In Psalm 18, he gives glory to God for rescuing him and using him in spite of opposition from those who hated him. The title of the psalm indicates David did not count Saul among his enemies. If other people consider us their enemies, we have every right to protect ourselves, but we must not treat them as enemies. We must obey Jesus (Matt. 5:38–48) and pray the way He prayed (Luke 23:34). Deliverance is one of the key themes in Psalm 18 (vv. 2–3, 16–17, 19, 43, 48), and it describes the many trials David experienced during those painful years when Saul was pursuing him in the wilderness of Judea.

David's years as a fugitive were especially difficult. The wilderness of Judea was certainly not the most pleasant place to live. It was hot and arid, rocky and desolate, a wasteland of caves, hills, and mountains. David had a small army of loyal and skilled men traveling with him (1 Sam. 22:2). Imagine providing food and water for four hundred men, covering your tracks, and living in rocky crags and caves just to survive. But David trusted the Lord, and He protected him and his men and provided for them. The many aspects of nature mentioned often in David's psalms no doubt grew out of his years as a shepherd in a pasture and a fugitive in a desert.

David had his share of family problems. Saul was not only David's king but also his father-in-law, and it pained David deeply that Saul wanted to kill him. Even his wife Michal, Saul's younger daughter, criticized him (2 Sam. 6:16–23). Three of his sons—Absalom, Amnon, and Adonijah—gave him great grief. Amnon raped his half-sister Tamar and was killed by Absalom. Absalom engineered a civil war and tried to take the throne from David and was slain in the process. During David's last days, Adonijah attempted to snatch the crown from Solomon and also take David's nurse, Abishag, as his wife. Solomon had him killed. David had more than eight wives and many concubines, plus more than twenty sons and daughters, and he wasn't always the best father or disciplinarian. Had he obeyed Deuteronomy 17:17, he might have avoided much sorrow.

David also suffered for his own sins, especially committing adultery with Bathsheba (2 Sam. 11–12) and taking a census of the people (2 Sam. 24). David's guilt and shame compounded after his dealings with Bathsheba and Uriah, her husband, and by the time Nathan the prophet arrived to confront David, a year had already passed (2 Sam. 12). In the process, David penned the words to Psalm 51 and has since been a model for humility and repentance for us. David always confessed his sins and accepted God's chastening. We learn from David that what distinguishes the best of God's people isn't that they are perfect but that they are forgiven.

There isn't a burden we carry, a pain we feel, or a battle we fight that isn't dealt with somewhere in the Bible, especially in the life and writings of David. Each time I have faced a decision or a satanic attack, the Lord has always given me just the promise I have needed. "God's way is perfect. All the LORD's promises prove true. He is a shield for all who look to him for protection" (Ps. 18:30).

1. List the word pictures that David employs in Psalm 18 to describe God and God's deliverances. What encouragement do these provide when we must deal with enemies?
2. What do you think David meant when he wrote, "Your *gentleness* has made me great" (v. 35 NKJV)?

Day 36

David: The Singer

Read Psalms 19; 119:49–56

Whenever we turn to the book of Psalms for spiritual help, we ought to thank the Lord for using David and others to write these hymns *and for sustaining them during the severe trials they experienced so they could write them.* Of course, some of his suffering David brought on himself, because the Lord always chastens those He loves (Heb. 12:1–13), but David profited from the chastening and did not give up. Nobody could write Psalm 23 who was unfamiliar with the hills and valleys of the life of faith and the dangers we meet when we don't stay near the Shepherd. The psalm speaks of burdens as well as blessings, fears as well as faith. The messianic psalms, especially Psalm 22, remind us that David experienced some of Christ's sufferings before our Lord even came to earth.

David arose early in the morning and started his day praising the Lord. "Wake up, lyre and harp! I will wake the dawn with my song" (Ps. 108:2; see also 57:8). David not only sang *about* the Lord, but he also sang *to* the Lord and worshipped Him. The first thought of his day wasn't about his to-do list or his needs but passionate praise of God! No wonder David was called "the sweet psalmist [singer] of Israel" (2 Sam. 23:1).

Psalm 19 tells us that David rejoiced in God's creation around him and above him (vv. 1–6). Even though selfish people have mutilated and wasted God's creation, we can still behold His glory and be awed by His wisdom as we look at the heavens by day or by night. We boast that we have sent men to the moon, but we forget that God ordained the movements of the heavenly bodies and the mathematics that made it possible for astronauts to journey to the moon and return safely.

David knew not only how to weep in the night (Ps. 30:5) but also how to sing "songs in the night" (Job 35:10; see also Ps. 42:8). Anyone can sing in the sunshine, but it takes faith in the Lord and love for Him to sing when everything seems dark. Paul and Silas sang in jail in the nighttime, and their song brought the jailer to his knees, and he was saved (Acts 16:25–34). Prayer changes things, and so does praise! It was late in the evening when the Lord Jesus sang in the upper room with His disciples the night He was betrayed (Matt. 26:30).

"I reflect at night on who you are, O LORD" (Ps. 119:55). I have often been awakened in the night and, as I meditated on the Word, the Lord has taught me precious truths (Ps. 19:7–11). But He has also tested and examined me in the night (Ps. 17:3), and I have had to confess sin and seek His forgiveness. "I lie awake thinking of you," David wrote, "meditating on you through the night. Because you are my helper, I sing for joy in the shadow of your wings" (Ps. 63:6–7). These wings belonged to the cherubim on the cover of the ark, spreading their wings in the holy of holies of the tabernacle. Under the shadow of His wings is the safest place in the world!

Whether it was in a cave or a palace, in the morning sun or the midnight hour, the nearness of God brought a song out of David's heart. Using Paul's words, let us do as David did: "Sing psalms and hymns and spiritual songs to God with thankful hearts" (Col. 3:16).

1. What songs are important to your life and faith?
2. Try to write a song of praise to God based on Psalm 19.

Day 37

David: The Successful

Read 1 Samuel 17

A dead lion defeated Samson the judge, but living lions and bears prepared David to become the most successful king in Israel's history. Our Lord often uses difficult and even dangerous experiences to prepare us to serve others and to achieve greater things. When King Saul died on the battlefield, he left the Jewish nation in shambles, but God enabled David to make wise decisions and restore national pride and order. How did David acquire such courage and skill? By caring for his father's sheep and goats and confronting and overcoming the lions and bears that attacked them.

When it came to Goliath, whose name means "splendor," David saw an enemy of Israel masquerading in light and threatening the glory of God. "The LORD who rescued me from the claws of the lion and the bear will rescue me from this Philistine," David told Saul (1 Sam. 17:37), and the Lord did just that. David challenged Goliath, not because Goliath was a giant but because he blasphemed the name of the God of Israel. We might choose to fight battles for the accolades we will receive, but it was God's splendor that burdened David most.

Two armies saw David kill Goliath, but only God saw him kill the predators that attacked his father's flocks. These hidden victories were dress rehearsals for slaying Goliath, for God usually prepares His servants in private before He presents them in public. David was ready to face Goliath because he allowed God to train him and test him without the encouragement of cheerleaders and spectators. If we are submissive and obedient in the private experiences of life, we will do a better job when God opens the curtains and we find ourselves on center stage.

The book of Proverbs uses lions as a way to distinguish the lazy from the bold. "The lazy person claims, 'There's a lion on the road! Yes, I'm sure there's a lion out there!'" (26:13; see also 22:13). But because David was a faithful shepherd, he faced the enemy courageously and protected the flock. "The wicked run away when no one is chasing them, but the godly are as bold as lions" (Prov. 28:1). The problem is not that lions exist but whether we will be courageous in our own private lives to fight against them for the sake of godliness. In the end, it was David's, not Goliath's, that was a life of splendor, because he boldly acted on the Lord's promises.

Some of the greatest leaders in history invested time preparing themselves privately so they would be ready when their opportunities came. The people God prepares don't look for opportunities; the opportunities look for them. Benjamin Disraeli, twice British prime minister, said, "The secret of success in life, is for a man to be ready for his opportunity when it comes."[1] All of life is preparation for the next thing God has prepared for us, and we must be alert to see the open doors and walk through them. If we delay, the door may close and the opportunity be lost forever.

William Arthur Ward said, "Adversity causes some men to break; others, to break records."[2] David broke records when his opportunities came because he used the tough times and the rough experiences to prepare himself for what God had prepared for him (Eph. 2:10). Today's challenges are tomorrow's victories. We should not hide or live in fear but boldly move forward in faith and do what is right in the eyes of the Lord. This is the secret to a splendid life.

1. Saul and Israel's army faced the Philistines for forty days as Goliath issued his challenge. The Israelites considered geography, the numbers of soldiers, and tactics—and feared. David raised another factor to the highest priority—and won. Look back at the reading and see what that was.

2. God builds our courage in private to fight the battles in public. Are you becoming newly courageous? How might God use that?

Benaiah: The King's Soldier

Read 2 Samuel 23:2–23; 1 Peter 5:1–11

Benaiah was one of David's top four soldiers who helped guard the king (1 Kings 1:38). He was born into a priestly family (1 Chron. 27:5) but spent his life as a valiant soldier, serving both David and Solomon. He met and defeated all kinds of enemies, but the one victory that stands out to me is that "on a snowy day, he chased a lion down into a pit and killed it" (2 Sam. 23:20). The prolific Englishman-turned-Australian preacher and writer Frank W. Boreham wrote that it was "bad enough ... to fight a lion; but a lion in a pit! And a lion in a pit on a snowy day!"[1] He faced the worst of enemies in the worst of places under the worst of conditions—and won! That's great fighting, and great preaching!

But before Benaiah won the battles attributed to him, he had to win the battle of God's calling for his life. He was born into a priestly family and could have had a much safer and easier life at the sanctuary of God, but he had great courage and exceptional gifts as a soldier. His family must have agreed with him, because there is no record that anybody stood in the way of his military career. Is the military life a holy calling like the priestly life? David and Solomon thought so, and so did the Lord, because the Lord gave Benaiah victory in many situations. He protected both David and Solomon and was an example of valor to soldiers of much lower rank.

Old Christian hymns such as "Onward, Christian Soldiers" and "The Son of God Goes Forth to War" represent an era when militant songs were sung in the church. Whether we like it or not, the Christian life involves battles as well as blessings, and if the church lays down its spiritual weapons and armor (Eph. 6:10–18) and chooses to ignore Paul's cry "Fight the good fight for the true faith" (1 Tim. 6:12), we will be slaughtered by our enemies. As a Christian, I belong to "a Kingdom of priests" (Rev. 1:6), but I am also to "endure suffering ... as a good soldier of Christ Jesus" (2 Tim. 2:3). There are many military metaphors in Scripture, and in these difficult days we need to pay attention to them.

That Benaiah "chased" (v. 20) the lion suggests that he really had the lion on the run. Not only that, but Benaiah "went down" (v. 20 NASB1995) into the pit and killed the lion, which on a snowy day would be very risky. One slip and the lion is upon you. For a soldier to chase a lion and the lion to flee to a pit is a remarkable scenario. After all, a cornered, angry lion is hardly the safest company. We need more people like Benaiah who will risk their lives to make things safer for the rest of us (Rom. 16:4).

Christians are in the Lord's army, fighting against the enemies of the faith. Our weapons are spiritual, and if we use them in the Spirit's power, they are effective. Each morning, I put on the armor of God by faith, piece by piece, and I use the sword and shield during the day when the Enemy attacks. It makes a difference! No matter how Satan the lion attacks us (1 Pet. 5:8–9), we must not back down but be priestly warriors who wield "the sword of the Spirit, which is the word of God" (Eph. 6:17). Benaiah proves that, pit or no pit, snow or no snow, "overwhelming victory is ours through Christ, who loved us" (Rom. 8:37).

1. How does it sit with you to be called a soldier in the Lord's army? Are you prepared to stand your ground in the Lord?

2. Is it a daily habit yet to pray on the armor of God (Eph. 6:10–18)?

Day 39

God Does What He Pleases

Read Psalm 135

No believer would ever question the fact that the Lord is *good* (v. 3), *great* (v. 5), *generous* (v. 12), and *glorious* (vv. 13–14). But have we ever questioned whether the Lord knows what He is doing? "The LORD does whatever pleases him throughout all heaven and earth, and on the seas and in their depths" (v. 6).

Moses thought God was making a mistake when He called him to lead His people out of Egypt (Ex. 3–4). Joshua was sure God made a mistake when He allowed Israel to be defeated when they attacked Ai, and he prayed until evening for help (Josh. 7). David wondered if God was mistaken when He permitted King Saul to pursue him year after year. The young man Jeremiah thought the Lord was making a big mistake by calling him to be a prophet (Jer. 1), and Peter was sure Jesus was mistaken when He put Calvary on the agenda (Matt. 16:21–28). A few years later, Peter told the Lord He was mistaken when He commanded him to eat unclean food (Acts 10).

"Our God is in the heavens, and he does as he wishes" (Ps. 115:3). Job 23:13 says it even more bluntly: "But once he has made his decision, who can change his mind? Whatever he wants to do, he does." This means, not that God is inconsistent and inconsiderate, but that He is free to work His own will as He sees fit. His character does not change; in fact, it is His unchangeable attributes that give Him the freedom to act as He does. Because He knows everything, is active everywhere, and can do anything, He is free to exercise His own will for our good and His glory.

We might be worried or even frightened because God always has His own way, except for one thing: the reality of God's eternal love. "The counsel of the LORD stands forever, the plans of His heart from generation to generation" (Ps. 33:11 NASB1995). God called Moses because He loved him and wanted to magnify His name through him. God allowed Joshua to be defeated temporarily by the people of Ai so that he might discover Achan the sinner and prevent future failures. David's years as a fugitive molded him into a great general and an even greater king. On and on it goes: "And we know that God causes everything to work together for the good of those who love God and are called according to his purpose for them" (Rom. 8:28).

When circumstances baffle us and we think God has made a mistake, remember the cross of Jesus Christ. It looked like a mistake to Peter and his friends and a victory for the Enemy, but it meant the defeat of Satan, the redemption of sinners, and the fulfillment of God's perfect plan. Paul boasted in the cross (Gal. 6:14), and so should we! From the human viewpoint, our Lord's arrest and death were unthinkable, inhuman crimes, but they led to the resurrection of the Lord Jesus Christ, His ascension, and His present ministry as High Priest.

One of my seminary professors called the cross of Christ "that great plus sign on the skyline," and it is. It looked like everything had come apart, but the cross brought it all together. The Lord does whatever He pleases because He knows what He is doing! Is there a prayer God hasn't answered yet? God can be trusted. Is there a hope unrealized you are still holding closely? It may seem to us like God's made a mistake or cares little. Take heart, for God is good, great, generous, and glorious.

1. How does God's character as good, great, generous, and glorious help you trust that He knows what He's doing?
2. Has there ever been a moment in your life when God has proven His character to you?
3. In what ways has Romans 8:28 comforted you?

Day 40

Truth Pleases God

Read Psalm 51

The God we worship is not only "the living and true God" (1 Thess. 1:9) but also the "God of truth" (Deut. 32:4 NKJV) and the "Sovereign Lord, holy and true" (Rev. 6:10). His words and His works are true, and He is faithful in all He does and says. Jesus is the truth (John 14:6), the Holy Spirit is truth (1 John 5:6), and God's Word is truth (John 17:17). Note that the Godhead and the Word are not simply *true* but *truth*, the very essence of what is true. *Truth is what comprises reality, and the core of reality is God Himself.* As Paul explains in Romans 1:15–32, if we abandon God and His Word, we abandon truth itself and are destined to believe lies and worship false gods. From God's point of view, the history of the human race is not evolution from imperfection to perfection but devolution from truth to lies, from divine revelation to satanic deception.

Psalm 51 is King David's prayer of confession after he committed adultery with Bathsheba and arranged to have her husband killed. For months he tried to cover up his disobedience, but the Lord knew what he was doing and sent the prophet Nathan to confront him. David confessed his guilt (2 Sam. 12) and was forgiven; however, he was also disciplined by the Lord and paid dearly for his sins.

"But you desire honesty from the womb" (Ps. 51:6), said David, echoing what he said in Psalm 15:1–2: "Who may worship in your sanctuary, LORD? Who may enter your presence on your holy hill? Those who lead blameless lives and do what is right, speaking the truth from sincere hearts." It is possible to say something with our lips that we don't really mean in our hearts. "Dear children, let's not merely say that we love each other; let us show the truth by our actions" (1 John 3:18). David could have offered many sacrifices, but he knew the Lord wanted truth and repentance (Ps. 51:16–19). He remembered what Samuel told King Saul when Saul lied about his "obedience" and offered sacrifices: "What is more pleasing to the LORD: your burnt offerings and sacrifices or your obedience to his voice? Listen! Obedience is better than sacrifice, and submission is better than offering the fat of rams" (1 Sam. 15:22).

If we want to please God, we must orient our lives around the truth. God's truth directs us (Ps. 25:5) and protects us (Ps. 91:4), and without it, we are wanderers in a desert. "Make them holy by your truth," Jesus prayed. "Teach them your word, which is truth" (John 17:17). The first part of our spiritual armor that is named is "the belt of truth" (Eph. 6:14), and since the belt holds things together, we could say "the belt of integrity." Truth must be defended or it will be lost (Ps. 45:4), and the best way to defend it is to practice it.

God is pleased when His people read and study the truth and seek to obey it, no matter what the cost. "Get the truth and never sell it" (Prov. 23:23). In spite of the claims of some philosophers and theologians, *there is such a thing as the truth and the truth can be sold!* How? By knowing the truth but refusing to obey it and defend it. The word *act* is a key part of the word *character* because we build character by the way we act as well as by what we believe. We please God and develop our own character when we love the truth and seek to live it.

1. In Psalm 51 David both confesses (vv. 3–4) his sin and repents (v. 17) of it. What is the distinction between confession and repentance? Why are both necessary to becoming new?
2. What challenges to biblical truth are being raised in our world today? How do you respond?

Day 41

Worship Pleases God

Read Psalm 95

Worship doesn't please God for the same reasons applause pleases performers or cheers please athletes. God needs neither affirmation nor encouragement. Worship pleases Him because of what it says about the worshippers and what it does for them. When we worship, we are loving and obeying God and opening our inner being to Him. In true worship, we surrender ourselves and our circumstances and focus on the greatness and glory of God. We yield ourselves to Him and submit to His perfect will. In prayer, we look up and tell Him our needs, but in worship, we bow down in awe and acknowledge His majesty and glory. This is a cleansing and a maturing experience that brings joy to the Father's heart as He sees His children grow in grace. It also prevents us from drifting into idolatry and paying more attention to the gifts than the Giver.

Whether alone or with others, when we come to the throne of grace in heaven's Most Holy Place, the Spirit of God uses the Word to cleanse and renew us (Heb. 10:19–25). We confess our sins, and the Father forgives us. He tells us (or reminds us) of tasks to be done and opportunities to seize, and we dedicate ourselves afresh to serving Him. During our working hours, we are conscious of time passing and tasks being completed, but when we worship, we center in on God and are bathed in the eternal and grow hungry for greater holiness in our lives. Just as parents appreciate fellowship with their children and that fellowship deepens as the children mature, so the Father is pleased when His children devote time to fellowshipping with Him. The Father loves His Son, Jesus Christ, and the more we become like Jesus, the deeper is our experience of God's love—and the opposition of the world.

Worship is not just an occasion for adoring God, although that is certainly primary; it is also a time for us to become new. One of the greatest joys of worship is having the Spirit teach us truths from the Word that encourage, transform, and edify us. "When your words came, I ate them; they were my joy and my heart's delight, for I bear your name, LORD God Almighty" (Jer. 15:16 NIV). Ignoring God's Word and being in a hurry to read and to pray are the two greatest enemies of a satisfying devotional life. There is something seriously wrong with our priorities if we can't "take time to be holy."

The angels in heaven are perfect. They are stronger than we are, and they live and serve in the presence of the Lord. *But God cannot have the kind of fellowship with angels that He can have with us!* Jesus did not become an angel; He became a human being just like us, only without sin. He did it so that He might save us and give us the privilege of communion with Him and the Father through the Spirit and the Word (Heb. 2:14–18). Worship must never be reduced to music or a stage. Our song forever is Jesus, who on the cross of Calvary purchased so great a salvation to redeem us.

When we gather as God's people, we please God and we are blessed. Worship is not "a part of the Christian life"; it is the very essence of the Christian life, just as breathing is to our physical life. Worship makes service a delight, the Christian life an adventure, and bearing burdens a privilege.

1. What emotions do you find in Psalm 95 as His people worship God?
2. What's one gift you've received from God that you can take time today to appreciate Him as the Giver of?

Day 42

Prayer Pleases God

Read Psalm 66:16–20; John 15:1–7

Why would God delight in hearing us pray? After all, He knows our needs far better than we do (Matt. 6:8), and He knows what we will say even before we speak (Ps. 139:4). So, why pray? *We pray because prayer is God's appointed way for us to receive what He wants to give us and because being able to pray effectively means that we are right with God and others.* When our Lord was serving here on earth, He began early each morning by praying to the Father and receiving His orders for the day (Mark 1:35; Isa. 50:4–5). We should follow His example.

In order to pray effectively, we must have faith, for "it is impossible to please God without faith" (Heb. 11:6). In order to have faith, we must be growing in God's Word (Rom. 10:17), abiding in God's love (John 15:7), and obeying God's will. "If I had cherished sin in my heart, the Lord would not have listened" (Ps. 66:18 NIV). The word *cherished* means "to know that sin is there *and to approve of it*." If we cherish sin, we grieve the Father, who at least a dozen times in the Scriptures says, "You shall be holy." We also grieve the Lord Jesus, who shed His blood to open the way into God's presence so that we might be able to pray (Heb. 10:19), and we grieve the Holy Spirit, who dwells within us and intercedes for us (Rom. 8:26–27).

Effective prayer involves praying in the will of God. In his book *The Tests of Life*, Robert Law writes, "Prayer is a mighty instrument, not for getting man's will done in Heaven, but for getting God's will done in Earth."[1] The apostle John agrees: "This is the confidence which we have before Him, that, if we ask anything according to His will, He hears us. And if we know that He hears us in whatever we ask, we know that we have the requests which we have asked from Him" (1 John 5:14–15 NASB1995). Prayer helps us know and do God's will.

In Matthew 5:21–26, Jesus explains that we are not fit to worship and pray if there is an unresolved conflict in the heart. That must be settled first, and then we can talk to the Father. We must leave the sacrifice at the altar and go to the person and resolve the problem, for "obedience is better than sacrifice" (1 Sam. 15:22). Years ago, as I was preparing a message, deep conviction was hindering me because I remembered a disagreement I had with a brother. I couldn't go see him personally, but I phoned him and settled the matter, and then the Lord helped me prepare the message. First Peter 3:7 says that this principle also applies to married couples.

Because the psalmist had confessed his sin (Ps. 66:18), he had a testimony to share with others about God's powerful answer to his prayer (vv. 16–20). God listens when we pray, and He hears more than just our words. He pays attention and responds as only God can. Prayer not only meets our needs, but it also measures our spirituality and helps us discover the areas in our lives that need attention. If we ignore this important part of becoming new, we will become careless, for prayer is both the thermostat and the thermometer of the Christian life. If the temperature has dipped, it's time to get on our knees.

1. One reason for keeping a prayer list is to have a record of God's answers. Do you have a prayer list?
2. What answers to those prayers are causing you to praise God?

Day 43

Obedience Pleases God

Read Psalm 119:1–16; John 15:9–17

Obedience is not an option God gives us to consider; it's an obligation He expects us to fulfill. "Never think that Jesus commanded a trifle," said D. L. Moody, "nor dare to trifle with anything he has commanded."[1] According to Jesus, obedience puts a foundation under our feet so that no storm can destroy the life He has enabled us to build (Matt. 7:24–29). Fair-weather Christians do their own thing in their own way and are unprepared for the inevitable tests of life. It is the obedient Christians who weather the storms and are strengthened.

God provides fathers and mothers in homes to protect their children, provide for them, and prepare them for adulthood, and submission to authority is a major part of the family curriculum. Children who don't learn to obey at home will not easily learn the other important lessons of life. This also applies to recruits in the armed forces, students in school, and athletes on a sports team. Ultimately, a child who doesn't obey his or her parents will hardly want to obey God!

There are certain motivations for obedience. Next to not obeying at all, the lowest level of living is to obey out of fear of punishment. We obey or—consequences! A slightly better motivation is to obey because we receive some kind of reward. Yes, there are benefits to obedience, but they are *benefits* and not *bribes*. The highest level is to obey because it makes us joyful and pleases those who command us. "Joyful are those who obey his laws" (Ps. 119:2). The joy of obedience far outweighs avoiding discipline or receiving payment. "How can a young person stay pure? By obeying your word" (v. 9). The benefits of obedience go beyond simply completing a task. Our obedience honors the Lord, those to whom we are responsible, and those we serve. Obeying God produces a holy life.

God doesn't owe us anything. The fact that Christ died to save us ought to be motivation enough for us to obey. But the Lord has graciously seen fit to bless us and reward us when we do His will! Jesus obeyed the Father because of love (John 15:10), and love motivates our obedience to Jesus (vv. 9–10). When you love someone, you *want* to obey. Jesus further emphasized that obedience results in overflowing joy (v. 11).

"You are my friends if you do what I command" (v. 14). Jesus said that ... and it's no trifle.

1. What qualities of an obedient child of God found in Psalm 119:1–16 is God developing in you?
2. When it comes to obedience, there are two little words that reveal our attitude. Look closely at Psalm 119:8, 15, and 16. What are they?

Day 44

Pure Words Please God

Read Psalms 12; 19:14; James 3:1–12

The wise man said, "The LORD detests evil plans, but he delights in pure words" (Prov. 15:26). The prophet said the Lord listens to what we say to one another (Mal. 3:16), a truth that ought to frighten liars and gossips. Yet what Jesus says ought to sober us completely: He says our words will one day be judged, for they reveal the nature of our hearts (Matt. 12:33–37). A word is just an utterance, but it carries tremendous power. The words of a doctor can save a life, and the words of a jury can send a person to prison. The right words printed in a book can inspire a person and unlock a future career. Wise words spoken in love can heal a broken heart. If we want to please the Lord, we must watch our words.

Let's begin with **the words we think** and the images that accompany them. Paul wrote, "Fix your thoughts on what is true, and honorable, and right, and pure, and lovely, and admirable. Think about things that are excellent and worthy of praise" (Phil. 4:8). Start thinking about a lie and you will give the Devil a foothold in your mind. Impure words and deeds each began as impure thoughts. Negative untrue thoughts about people can result in unkind words and actions and ruin a friendship or a marriage. Many people become paralyzed by fear of imaginary situations, which is why we must set our minds on Christ (Col. 3:2).

Jesus tells us that **the words we speak** come from our hearts, our inner beings (Matt. 12:34–35). If our hearts are clean and our motives pure, our words will be clean and pure, but if we secretly harbor malice and envy, our words can wound and kill. Contaminated words are a sign of a contaminated heart soured in a contaminated culture, which is why we must be aware of what we absorb from the world. Additionally, the words we *don't* say can do damage, especially when we have opportunities to express gratitude, give counsel, praise achievement, or share the gospel.

When we worship the Lord, we must be careful about **the words we sing.** Colossians 3:16 tells us that the worshipping congregation must sing *only that which is biblical.* A singer has no more right to sing a lie than a preacher has to preach a lie. Rather, the message of Christ ought to fill our hearts; then it will flow from our mouths. A few verses later, Paul tells the same believers, "Let your conversation be gracious and attractive so that you will have the right response for everyone" (Col. 4:6). An often-overlooked element of corporate worship is how we use our words to encourage one another (Heb. 10:25). We glorify God when we sing truth and remind one another of the gospel.

To another church, Paul instructed, "Don't use foul or abusive language. Let everything you say be good and helpful, so that your words will be an encouragement to those who hear them" (Eph. 4:29). "Obscene stories, foolish talk, and coarse jokes—these are not for you" (Eph. 5:4). Our words build our world, express our worship, and connect us to *the Word,* Jesus Himself (John 1:1). May the words of our mouths and the meditations of our hearts please the Lord today.

1. Memorize Psalm 19:14.
2. Public discourse has not changed from David's time to our time (Ps. 12). List the contrasts between human words and God's promises in this text. How often during a day do you allow yourself to be exposed to our culture's verbal bombardment?
3. Pray for God's help in controlling your tongue and becoming new with your words.

Generosity Pleases God

Read Psalm 112; 2 Corinthians 8:9–15

As I drove past a church sanctuary, the words on the outdoor sign caught my eye: "Christians are forgiven, forgiving, and FOR GIVING." That sentence says more than some sermons I have preached, but it deals with a topic that has never been popular. From cover to cover, the Bible deals with the subject of giving and repeatedly encourages generosity.

This is obviously true because **our heavenly Father is generous**. If we received an annual bill from the Lord for all the sunshine and rain, beauty and food, strength and health He provides, we would not be able to pay it. He built into His creation all that we need, from birth to death, and gave us the ability to enjoy it (1 Tim. 6:17). He gives us the people we need in our lives, such as doctors and nurses, grocers, mechanics, and teachers, and the income we need to pay our bills (Deut. 8:12–18). How we ought to thank Him, for "he gives his sunlight to both the evil and the good, and he sends rain on the just and the unjust alike" (Matt. 5:45).

But even more, He gave His beloved Son to die for our sins, and He forgives us and makes us His children when we receive Jesus as our Lord and Savior. His invitation is not "Do" or "Pay" or "Try" but simply "Come!" He has "blessed us with every spiritual blessing in the heavenly realms because we are united with Christ" (Eph. 1:3). The Lord has given us His Word, and it is our light, our nourishment, our sword, and our greatest treasure. He has given us the Holy Spirit, the privilege of prayer, the fellowship of the church, and the hope of heaven.

Christians don't just celebrate the generosity of God but remember **others have been generous to us.** When Paul received the gifts sent from the believers in Philippi, he saw them as "a sweet-smelling sacrifice that is acceptable and pleasing to God" (Phil. 4:18). How I thank God for family and friends who have encouraged and helped me in my life and ministry. When I was a young pastor, older pastor friends shared their valuable time with me and counseled me about the best books to read and the best ways to work with people in the church, and they enriched me. Paul's admonition to the church in Corinth was to give to others out of their plenty in this high season and receive from others in low seasons. This is part of fellowship in the body of Christ!

How do we show we are grateful for God's generosity? **We generously give back to God and to others.** "And this same God who takes care of me will supply all your needs from his glorious riches, which have been given to us in Christ Jesus" (Phil. 4:19). That promise was not given to every Christian; it was given to those who, like the Philippian believers, give generously to the Lord. This doesn't mean we are paying God to bless us. It means we are proving to God by our giving that He can trust us with His blessings. Those who have the grace to give also have the grace to receive and to use every gift to the glory of God. In Psalm 112, "those who fear the LORD" (v. 1) "are generous" (v. 4) and "give generously to those in need" (v. 9).

God owns everything. He generously gives to us so that we can be generous to others. Jesus is our example: "For you know the grace of our Lord Jesus Christ, that though He was rich, yet for your sakes He became poor, that you through His poverty might become rich" (2 Cor. 8:9 NKJV).

1. Memorize Deuteronomy 8:18.

2. When you give your offering at your church, do you feel like you're paying a bill or tipping God? Or do you have a sense of celebration in honoring God's faithfulness to you?

3. Is there a shame or insecurity you feel around money? Ask God to open your heart and hands to use you generously in the lives of people around you.

Day 46

Perspective Pleases God

Read Psalm 73

Asaph wrote this psalm after winning a difficult spiritual battle. He had stopped walking by faith and was beginning to envy his proud, prosperous neighbors who ignored God but seemed to be successful in all they did (vv. 1–12). Then he looked at himself and decided he was stupid to live for the Lord, for his neighbors had more than enough, while he was often in trouble (vv. 13–14). He didn't talk to anybody about his dilemma, which was a good thing because he would have ended up almost blaspheming God (v. 15). Instead, he got smart and went to the house of God and told the Lord how he felt. As he focused his faith on the Lord, his heart was calmed. He pondered the judgments that would come to unbelievers as well as the blessings he had received from the Lord (vv. 16–28). The next time you get "out of focus," ponder these blessings and let them reframe your perspective.

The Lord holds us because we belong to Him (v. 23). This echoes the words of Solomon's bride, who said, "I am my lover's, and my lover is mine" (Song 6:3). In the wilderness, David wrote, "I cling to you; your strong right hand holds me securely" (Ps. 63:8). The Christian belongs to God because of Christ. "God bought you with a high price" (1 Cor. 6:20), with "the precious blood of Christ, the sinless, spotless Lamb of God" (1 Pet. 1:19).

The Lord guides us so we can enjoy Him, serve Him, and glorify Him (v. 24). It's too bad when a wedding is treated like the finish line to a dating relationship instead of the starting line to a lifelong, maturing love. In our relationship with Christ, we are made new day by day. As we abide in Christ, we grow deeper in our love for Him, for the better we know Him, the more we love Him. His desires become our desires, and we serve Him without complaint, and this glorifies the Lord. "Loving God means keeping his commandments, and his commandments are not burdensome" (1 John 5:3). As day by day we follow Jesus, our Savior and Lord, He leads us to "a glorious destiny" (Ps. 73:24)—the Father's house (John 14:1–6).

The Lord satisfies us (vv. 25–28). The Christian life is an adventure of enjoying the Lord and His blessings! "Since you have been raised to new life with Christ, set your sights on the realities of heaven, where Christ sits in the place of honor at God's right hand" (Col. 3:1). Physically we are on earth, but spiritually we are in heaven, where Jesus is enthroned (Eph. 2:4–7). By His Spirit, Jesus is in us and with us here on earth to provide everything we need. "As He is, so are we *in this world*" (1 John 4:17 NKJV). What we have in heaven is worth far more than all we have on earth, or anything we may lose on earth, because we serve Christ!

It's often said that some Christians are so heavenly minded that they're no earthly good. The cure for that sin is for us to rejoice in all we have *now* in Christ in heaven and draw upon those riches by faith. This is how we serve others and glorify God. God's people have the best of both worlds! Jesus came down and linked heaven and earth. That wonderful link continues and is strengthened in our lives every time we pray, "May your will be done on earth, as it is in heaven" (Matt. 6:10). Set your affection and attention on things above, and you will experience transformation miracles here below.

1. In verses 13–14, Asaph is asking God if it's worth it to follow Him. Have you ever asked this of God? What was the circumstance?

2. Asaph starts to get life in the right perspective in verse 17. What habit does this suggest is necessary for God's people?

Day 47

Dependence Pleases God

Read Psalm 16

As a young man, I went off to seminary in Chicago, and the first week I prayed, "Lord, help me not to waste my opportunity. Please give me a verse that will carry me through my studies." I truly believe God honored this prayer of dependence, because He spoke to me in the last verse of Psalm 16: "You will show me the path of life; in Your presence is fullness of joy; at Your right hand are pleasures forevermore" (v. 11 NKJV). While I had great instructors who helped me grow a hunger for God's Word, it was this verse that anchored my faith and dependence upon God. Three times in this psalm, David highlights our dependence upon the Lord and the assurances we have if we follow Him by faith.

The Lord is my goodness. Some translations begin this psalm with the word *preserve*. I admit there have only been a few times that I have had to ask God to preserve my life. In the midst of them, I, like David, have found comfort in the truth that God is good and He is *my* goodness (v. 2 NKJV). Regardless of our circumstances, our goodness is God. Whenever I open my hands and receive a blessing, I know it's come from His hand. And whenever I have withstood the temptations of life, I know it's because the Lord has been my goodness (v. 8).

The Lord is my gladness. Faith in God causes our hearts to be glad, our tongues to rejoice, and our bodies to rest in hope (v. 9). Peter quoted this

136

verse when he preached the first sermon at Pentecost and applied these words to Jesus (Acts 2:25–28). The resurrection of Jesus from the dead is a reality that should bring a hopeful gladness to the hearts of believers. How sad it is when Christians forget our Lord has defeated the grave! At the graveside we do not mourn like those who do not have hope (1 Thess. 4:13). This doesn't mean that we don't feel emotions or process grief; rather, the believer's hope is grounded in God's good work in Christ. Therefore, we can be glad in all things.

The Lord is my guide (v. 11). During my life, I have tested this verse and found no reason to doubt that God has a definite plan for His children. As a teenager I memorized Ephesians 2:8–9, but verse 10 carries equal importance: "For we are God's masterpiece. He has created us anew in Christ Jesus, so we can do the good things he planned for us long ago." By faith, we can trust Him to show us the path to walk, and He will. God's path always leads to God's presence. God never promised us an easy life, but He did promise to be with us. Matthew's gospel opens with the name of Jesus, "Immanuel ... God is with us" (1:23), and closes, "And be sure of this: I am with you always, even to the end of the age" (28:20).

The presence of God and the joy that comes with Him as my guide brings tremendous pleasure. Don't fall into the misbelief that the Christian life is only misery and suffering. Our Father "richly gives us all we need for our enjoyment" (1 Tim. 6:17). The Lord guides us so that we might enjoy Him and the life He gives. The best part is that it will never end! God's path will one day lead to His glorious presence—heaven! And there in heaven we have pleasures forevermore.

1. Does your faith journey confirm that God is dependable? Scroll through your memory bank, and recall needs met, bodies healed, prayers answered, lives changed.

2. In Psalm 16, David was pointing ahead to the Messiah's victory over death. Jesus is alive! Have you ever lived as though Jesus were not alive?

3. Are you actively seeking God's guidance for yourself? Your family? Your work? Your church?

Day 48

The Case against Iniquity and Hypocrisy

Read Isaiah 1

"Hear ye! Hear ye! This court is now in session, the eternal almighty Lord God presiding!" That's the way Isaiah could have opened his book, because his first chapter is a courtroom scene. The citizens of the kingdom of Judah had rebelled against God and His law, and He was about to try them and pronounce them guilty. The prophet Isaiah lays out the charges against Judah and acts as the prosecuting attorney, speaking on behalf of Jehovah, the judge.

Iniquity: a nation full of sin (vv. 1–9, 21–23). His first indictment is that the nation was like children who had rebelled against their father (vv. 2–4). In His grace, the Lord had called them and made them His own. He had rescued them from bondage in Egypt, given them a fruitful land, and promised in His covenant to bless them if they obeyed Him. But they imitated the heathen nations around them and began to worship their gods. God had disciplined them to the point where their land was ruined and their whole "body politic" was sick (vv. 5–8). They would not repent and return to the Lord. Their idolatry was like prostitution (v. 21), and their character like cheap dross or diluted wine (v. 22).

Hypocrisy: a temple full of sinners (vv. 10–15). Isaiah compares Jerusalem to Sodom and Gomorrah, two of the wickedest cities named in Scripture, cities God destroyed (Gen. 18–19). He visits the temple and finds it filled with people bringing their sacrifices to the Lord! The people of Judah observed the special days and offered their expensive sacrifices, *and the Lord hated what they were doing!* Listen to what the Lord says: "I am sick of your burnt offerings.... I get no pleasure from the blood of bulls and lambs.... Stop bringing me your meaningless gifts.... Your special days ... are all sinful and false. I want no more of your pious meetings" (vv. 11–13). A full sanctuary or a lovely ceremony means nothing to the Judge *if our hearts are divided between the Lord and the idols of the world.* To attend services and then leave the temple for a place of sin is hypocrisy.

Opportunity: a Lord full of compassion (vv. 16–20, 24–31). What the people needed was to confess their sins and submit to the cleansing God offered them. "Wash yourselves" speaks of repentance and the putting away of sin. "Come now, let's settle this" is His invitation to all sinners. He promises to wash away their sins and restore them to His loving care. God in His mercy doesn't give us what we do deserve and in His grace does give us what we don't deserve! The Lord promises that "those who repent will be revived by righteousness" (v. 27). Righteousness is that quality of relationship devoid of fear or division. God's compassion would bridge the gap between Judah and Himself to heal the people and their land, but they continued to rebel and were eventually exiled in Babylon.

Can you see parallels between God's people then and God's people now? Are the crowds in the sanctuary of God because they love God and want to worship Him, or are they just covering up the sins they have committed? Or are they merely going through the motions? Jesus called the temple in His day "a den of thieves" (Matt. 21:13), the place where thieves hide after they have committed their crimes. Big crowds and generous gifts are not necessarily proof of devotion to God. "Obedience is better than sacrifice, and submission is better than offering the fat of rams" (1 Sam. 15:22). Ultimately, it took the sacrifice of our Savior to reveal righteousness apart from the law (Rom. 3:21). Isaiah later tells us it's by His wounds we are healed (53:5).

1. In verse 5, the prophet Isaiah asks Judah, "Must you rebel forever?" What does it mean to rebel against God?
2. In order for God to cleanse the sinful nation, what would the people have to admit? What does God do when sinners make that admission? Praise Jesus for doing this for you!

Day 49

Defining Our Terms

Read Isaiah 5:20–23; 59:9–15

God showed His wisdom when He gave names to things so they could be identified. Imagine how confused life would be if we lacked specific vocabulary words and had no basic language and grammar! By giving things names, God could teach our first parents how to live in the garden and what to do to please Him. It's important that we use both the right vocabulary and dictionary, and in a court of law a whole case can hang on the definition of a simple word. Isaiah convicts Israel on account of creative definitions. "What sorrow for those who say that evil is good and good is evil, that dark is light and light is dark, that bitter is sweet and sweet is bitter" (Isa. 5:20).

The apostle Peter warns us about false teachers with their "clever lies" (2 Pet. 2:3). The phrase "clever lies" sounds like "fake news," but it's literally "fabricated words." The word "fabricated" in the Greek is *plastos*, which gives us our word "plastic." Plastic words are words that can be molded and twisted to mean whatever you please. No one should use the words God has given us unless they use God's dictionary and the meanings He has given us.

The evening I was ordained into the ministry, the preacher gave a message based on Isaiah 59:14: "Truth is fallen in the street, and equity cannot enter" (KJV). He described the "traffic jams" in our world today because truth has been rejected. Years later I read George Orwell's novel *Nineteen Eighty-Four*, in which he introduced "doublethink," which means accepting as true two opposite concepts at the same time and seeing no contradiction.[1] During the sixties, "doublespeak" was introduced as a way to minimize some of the tragedies of modern life. The poor were called "fiscal underachievers," and bank robbery became "unauthorized withdrawals." Nobody admitted that soldiers were shot. Their wounds were "ballistically induced apertures in the subcutaneous environment." What could we say of today's era of "alternative facts"?

The Pharisees called their religious practices "holiness," but Jesus called it hypocrisy (Matt. 23). The high priests called their business activities in the temple "ministry," but Jesus said it was robbery (Matt. 21:13). The leaders of the church in Corinth called their treatment of an immoral member "toleration," but Paul said it was abomination. Diotrephes said he was a leader, but the apostle John said he was a dictator (3 John 9–10).

Real Christians don't write their own dictionaries; rather, they "speak the truth in love" (Eph. 4:15) and choose their words carefully. They avoid "doublespeak" and "plastic words" so people can understand them, and they heed Paul's admonition: "Let no one deceive you with empty words" (Eph. 5:6 NIV). God chose precisely the words He intended in Scripture. They do not need to be modified or updated.

In Lewis Carroll's *Through the Looking-Glass*, Humpty Dumpty says to Alice, "When *I* use a word ... it means just what I choose it to mean—neither more nor less."[2] He has many followers today. The "customs of this world" (Rom. 12:2) are to redefine language to our advantage. Followers of Jesus, on the other hand, obey Jesus's command: "Just say a simple, 'Yes, I will,' or 'No, I won't.' Anything beyond this is from the evil one" (Matt. 5:37). Perhaps this is what Jesus was noting when He saw Nathanael coming toward Him and remarked, "Now here is a genuine son of Israel—a man of complete integrity" (John 1:47). Some versions say, "in whom there is no deceit."

1. How do you use words? Are you tempted to reshape meaning to suit your conclusions?
2. How have you observed this temptation play out in society today?

At the Crossroads

Read Jeremiah 1; 6:16–20

Jeremiah was probably twenty years old when the Lord called him to leave the priesthood and become a prophet, a much more difficult vocation. A Jewish priest's work was somewhat routine, while a Jewish prophet was never sure what might happen next. Jeremiah's assignment was to continue Isaiah's ministry and call wayward Judah back to obedience to the Lord, for the Babylonian army was preparing to invade the land and punish the apostate nation.

Jeremiah entered into this calling without feeling adequate for the task. But God's calling always assures us of God's enabling. Although struggling with discouragement, Jeremiah served faithfully for forty years, suffered much, and watched the nation go into ruin and captivity. Imagine serving for forty years and seeming to accomplish nothing! But it wasn't his fault; it was the hard hearts of the people that brought about their own destruction. They wanted their own way, not God's way (Jer. 6:16), and they had to suffer the consequences of a bad choice. Israel was playing the fool when they should have grown in wisdom.

Wise people stop, look, and listen! Judah was definitely in a crossroads situation, and had the leaders listened to God's Word, they would have made the right decisions. They treated Jeremiah as an enemy when he was actually their best friend. As today, the false prophets were preaching lies and promising peace, but the storms were about to begin. "But the leaders, too, as one man, had thrown off God's yoke and broken his chains" (Jer. 5:5). When Jehudi read Jeremiah's prophecies to King Jehoiakim, the king cut the scroll with his knife and burned the Scripture in the fire (Jer. 36:20–26). Had the leaders stopped, looked around at the chaos the nation was in, listened to the prophet, and obeyed, God would have intervened.

Wise people ask for the old, godly way. One of the best ways for an individual believer or a church to go on a detour and lose God's blessing is to hunger for something new and novel. They want new ways to pray or new excuses not to pray, new ways to promote, new entertaining music and sermons—and in the end, it all fails. During my years of service, I have seen many "new and guaranteed" methods for ministry go up like rockets and come down like rocks, but the false prophets keep inventing them.

Wise people walk the old way in a new way. Once on the old, godly way, we don't stand still but move on with new faith and power. Transformation doesn't mean inventing clever new things or embalming the old things but returning humbly to God's way *with a new hunger for God.* The old becomes new when we have a fresh touch of the Spirit and a new devotion to the Word. When we repent and return to prayer and the Word of God and a desire to glorify Him, then the Lord can make the old things new and the new things of the world disgusting. As by faith we travel God's ancient path, we find rest, revival, and victory, and the Lord is honored.

At a crossroads we have to make a choice. "The LORD says: 'Stand at the crossroads and look; ask for the ancient paths, ask where the good way is, and walk in it, and you will find rest for your souls.' But you said, 'We will not walk in it'" (Jer. 6:16 NIV). Stop, look, listen, and obey. That's the way of wisdom—and the only way to becoming new!

1. Reach out to a wise saint about his or her walk with God, and ask if there's a quicker way to spiritual maturity. What does this teach you about the wisdom of the ancient path?

2. When your daily time with God becomes stale or routine, take steps to refresh it. Read from a different version of Scripture. Review your prayer list; then rewrite it. Relocate to a quieter or brighter spot. Journal the Scriptures, the daily reading, and your conversation with God. Make one of your prayer requests a renewed passion for God!

Day 51

The Cross-Examination

Read Jeremiah 6:10–15; 8:4–13

The kingdom of Judah did not suddenly trip and fall into judgment; for years it had been drifting away from its spiritual moorings and into the devastating storm about to break. The old-fashioned word for this experience of spiritual decline is *backsliding*, but it is not found in many modern versions of the Bible, having been replaced by *waywardness*, *unfaithfulness*, *wickedness*, and *apostasies*. "Return, faithless people; I will cure you of backsliding" (Jer. 3:22 NIV) is an invitation from the Lord that is worth taking seriously.

Consider the picture: Spiritual decline is like physical sickness. It begins secretly, sometimes preceded by an unbalanced diet, poor hygiene, or contact with somebody who is infectious. Then comes the gradual decline—loss of appetite, weariness, fever, pain, irritability, and general indisposition—followed by a sudden failure that forces us to the doctor, who may send us to bed or perhaps to the hospital. We might infect others, and if the disease is serious enough, we might be handicapped for life or even die. Medication, surgery, or special treatments can kill the germs or remove the tumors, but it still takes time to recover. I have had my share of surgeries, and I thank God for modern medicine, but I prefer to be healthy.

Listen to the promise: "I will heal!" There are some sick people who go through denial and will not admit they need help. "It will go away. I've been through it before." And sometimes it doesn't. Backslidden believers who will not face their sins and deal with them are robbing themselves of God's blessing and the privilege of serving others, and they could infect an entire church. As bad as that is, it's worse when people seek out a different diagnosis to find an easier treatment. There is a difference between getting a second opinion and seeking self-justification.

The false prophets in Jeremiah's day provided this, just as some unbiblical teachers do today. "They offer superficial treatments for my people's mortal wound. They give assurances of peace when there is no peace" (Jer. 6:14; see also 8:22). Our Lord examines us thoroughly, diagnoses us accurately, and heals us completely *if* we confess our sins and forsake them (Ps. 139:1–6, 23–24). Best of all, He pays the bill because "Christ died for our sins" (1 Cor. 15:3). We may suffer because of our disobedience—"Backsliders get what they deserve" (Prov. 14:14)—but Jesus paid the price for our "cure." We need no second opinions about that!

Respond to the Lord's plea and return: "Come back to Me." We should come back because of what our sins are doing to the Lord who died for us, to ourselves, and to those around us to whom we ought to be examples and servants. We rob ourselves when we stop walking daily with the Lord, when we're not being nourished by the Word, empowered and guided by the Spirit, or sharing Christ with others. His appeal comes from His heart of love because He wants the very best for us. "'For I know the plans I have for you,' says the LORD. 'They are plans for good and not for disaster, to give you a future and a hope'" (Jer. 29:11).

1. Jeremiah 8:4–7 indicates several signs of backsliding. These symptoms have a common cause, found in Jeremiah 6:10 and 8:9. Read these verses, and find both the cause and the cure for a backslidden soul.

2. What ultimately will happen to backsliders who do not reverse their course?

Day 52

Weighed in the Balance

Read Daniel 1; 6:10–13

Daniel, Hananiah, Mishael, and Azariah were exiled to Babylon after the fall of Jerusalem. They were gifted lads from noble families in the tribe of Judah—healthy, handsome, and at the head of their class (Dan. 1:17, 20). The Lord put them there to bear witness to the one true and living God. We will focus on Daniel, who, during a long and useful life, was promoted from one office to another. He was a dynamic leader whose life and witness made a significant contribution to the history of Israel, a balanced believer with the right priorities.

We should balance courage with tact. The authorities changed the young men's names to identify them with four Babylonian gods and then sent them to their schools to brainwash them. The leaders also provided a diet of foods that Jews were forbidden to eat. The four trainees had the courage to obey God's law, but they did it in such a way that neither they nor their supervisors got into trouble. Believers need not be belligerent, as the godly path often blesses the obedient believer as well as those who have yet to believe. "Let your conversation be gracious and attractive" (Col. 4:6).

We should balance the Word of God and prayer. Daniel opened his windows toward Jerusalem and prayed three times a day (Dan. 6:10). Even though the temple in Jerusalem had been destroyed, he was claiming the promise of 1 Kings 8:28–30. When he read Jeremiah 25:11–12, he turned God's promise into a fervent prayer of confession (Dan. 9:1–2). The early church balanced the Word with prayer (Acts 6:1–4), and so should we today. We don't look toward Jerusalem below but to the Savior above (Heb. 12:22–24). And we don't open a window, but we close the door (Matt. 6:5–6) and open our hearts.

We should balance opportunity and opposition. Daniel was a powerful official with great authority, and this aroused the envy and anger of the other advisers of the king. Even though Daniel saved the lives of the pagan wise men by explaining Nebuchadnezzar's dream (Dan. 2:24), they resented his skill and rejection of their gods. Chapter 6 describes their vicious plot to have Daniel killed, but the plot backfired and the accusers were slain. Opportunity and opposition usually go together (1 Cor. 16:9), and successful people are both honored and hated. Expect it.

We should balance weakness and strength. Seeing and then understanding the vision in Daniel 8 terrified Daniel and made him faint (vv. 15–18). The vision in chapter 10 terrified him and left him weak and pale (vv. 8–9, 19). The Lord strengthened His servant, but the experience was a difficult one. Paul reminds us that strength that knows itself to be strength is weakness but weakness that knows itself to be weakness is really strength (2 Cor. 12:1–10).

We should balance God's sovereignty with human responsibility. The book of Daniel as a whole emphasizes the sovereignty of God, but it also points out our part as intercessors, students, witnesses, and partners in serving the Lord. We work together with other believers as the Lord works in and through us. Meditating on Daniel 2:17–23 will increase your faith in a sovereign Lord who "controls the course of world events; he removes kings and sets up other kings" (v. 21). The early church prayed "O Sovereign Lord" (Acts 4:24), and so should we.

1. Daniel's loyalty to God and God's law made him a non-conformist: he refused the royal diet and he continued to pray. Are you feeling pressure to lower God's standards or be disloyal to Him? Pray for courage and a tactful approach.

2. Does your faith in Christ bring opposition from family members or coworkers? What encouragement do you find in Daniel's example?

3. Meditate on Daniel 2:17–23. How did Daniel know that God is real?

Day 53

A Character Witness

Read Haggai 1; Malachi 1

In the year 538 BC, about fifty thousand Jews left their captivity in Babylon and returned to their own land, where they hoped to rebuild Jerusalem and restore the worship of the Lord in their holy temple. They had godly leaders in Zerubbabel the governor, Joshua the high priest, and the prophets Haggai, Zechariah, and Malachi, but the hearts of most of the people were far from the Lord. When put on trial, the character of the people was found wanting. Times were difficult, but the situation would have improved if the nation had obeyed God's covenant and heeded the words God spoke to Solomon after the first temple was dedicated: "Then if my people who are called by my name will humble themselves and pray and seek my face and turn from their wicked ways, I will hear from heaven and will forgive their sins and restore their land" (2 Chron. 7:14).

The Lord brought His people back to their land so that they might honor His name (Mal. 2:2, 5; 3:16), but instead, they were showing contempt for His name (Mal. 1:6). The phrase "my name" is found ten times in Malachi, emphasizing the reason God brought them back to their land. Alas, the priests were neither giving godly leadership to the people nor setting a good example before them. They questioned God's love (Mal. 1:2), performed their duties in a perfunctory way (Mal. 1:13), and permitted the people to bring imperfect sacrifices to the altar, some of which were stolen (Mal. 1:7–14). In other words, neither the priests nor the people were giving their best to the Lord. God told them He would rather the temple doors were shut than that the people should worship Him in such a careless manner.

Yet the worshippers at the altar groaned and wept as though they were repenting and crying out for God's help, but He did not help them. He did not send rain, nor did He bless their fields and flocks (2:13–16). The men had been unfaithful to their wives and had divorced them to marry pagan women and worship pagan idols (2:11–16). The priests did not encourage the people to bring their tithes and offerings to the Lord (3:7–12), so there was little support for the ministry of the newly restored temple. They wanted God to bless them, yet they were robbing God. Does this state of affairs exist among God's leaders and people today?

How does God change this sad situation? "Behold, I send My messenger, and he will prepare the way before Me" (3:1 NKJV). The name Malachi means "my messenger," and the verse quoted refers to John the Baptist, who prepared the way for Jesus (4:5–6; Matt. 3; 11:7–10). God's Word warns us that Jesus is coming again and that we should be ready, not only as individual believers but also as churches (Rev. 2–3). Prepared believers are giving to the Lord faithfully and sacrificially and are seeking to honor His name before others. They serve Him heartily and "keep the doors open" so that God's people can worship and serve their Lord. They don't question God's love but love Him by obeying His commandments.

At least some of Malachi's hearers took action. "Those who feared the LORD spoke with each other, and the LORD listened to what they said. In his presence, a scroll of remembrance was written to record the names of those who feared him and always thought about the honor of his name" (Mal. 3:16). Those whom God is making new will demonstrate God's transforming power.

1. How do we know that God loves us? What actions support these words of God: "I have always loved you" (Mal. 1:2)? Read 1 John 4:9–17 to know how God loves you.

2. Are you giving God your best in all the relationships and activities of life?

3. Are you making progress in becoming a person who loves to think about God (Mal. 3:16)?

Interlude

As we begin our study of what the New Testament says about becoming new, please keep in mind that we are not abandoning the Old Testament. In the gospel of Matthew alone there are fifty-three quotations from the Old Testament as well as seventy-six allusions. The Old Testament was the only "Bible" the early church possessed, and by using it, they were able to evangelize the Roman Empire and build strong churches. Christ is found in the Old Testament in type and prophecy. Augustine said, "The New is in the Old concealed, the Old is by the New revealed."[1] They belong together and must not be separated.

Writing especially for Jewish readers, Matthew built the "bridge" between the Old and the New. He opens with a genealogy of Jesus that ties Him to the people and events of the Old Testament. In the Greek text of Matthew, the first sentence reads, "The book of the genesis of Jesus Christ, son of David, son of Abraham." With its genealogy and account of Christ's birth, this is the "Genesis" chapter of Matthew. Matthew 2 is the "Exodus" chapter, quoting Hosea 11:1: "I called my Son out of Egypt" (Matt. 2:15). The "Leviticus" chapter is Matthew 3, describing the ministry of John the Baptist, a priest called to be a prophet. Matthew 4 describes our Lord's temptation in the wilderness and is the "Numbers" chapter, for the book of Numbers describes Israel's wilderness trials. Matthew 5, 6, and 7 are what we know as the Sermon on the Mount. In this sermon, Jesus gives us a deeper understanding of God's law, just as Moses did in Deuteronomy (which means "second law"). We might say that chapters 1–7 of Matthew are the "Pentateuch" of the New Testament.

After the sermon, Jesus comes down from the mountain and meets a Jewish leper whom He cleanses by His grace and power. Then He heals the servant of a Roman officer, a Gentile, and His ministry of teaching and healing continues as He transforms minds, hearts, and bodies. *He is still empowering that kind of ministry, and you and I must be a part of it!* What our Lord "began to do and teach" (Acts 1:1), He continues to do and teach through His church by the power of His Holy Spirit (John 14:12).

Focus on our Lord Jesus Christ. He has so vividly revealed Himself to us as the Creator who brings order out of chaos, the Redeemer who transforms sinners into saints, the Enabler who turns weakness into strength, the Provider who meets every need, the Teacher who enlightens us, the Friend who encourages and comforts us, and the Shepherd who guides us. So we should pursue His work in us of becoming new and cooperate with His work through us to be transformers, by His grace. "Therefore, if anyone is in Christ, the new creation has come: The old has gone, the new is here!" (2 Cor. 5:17 NIV).

Hallelujah! The new is here! "Sing a new song to the LORD, for he has done wonderful deeds" (Ps. 98:1).

Part 2

In the New Testament

Day 54

The Son of God

Read John 1:1–5; Colossians 1:15–18; Hebrews 1:1–3

Jesus Christ, the eternal Son of God, our Savior and Lord, was with the Father and the Spirit in the creation work described in Genesis 1. "God created everything through him, and nothing was created except through him" (John 1:3). Not only did Jesus share in creation, but today He "sustains everything by the mighty power of his command" (Heb. 1:3). In the original Greek text, the word translated as "sustains" describes three vital ministries of our Savior: He is holding everything up so it won't collapse, He is holding everything together so it functions properly, and He is carrying everything along to fulfill its ultimate purpose. Without Jesus Christ, there could be no creation, no full revelation of the Father (John 14:1–11), no good news of redemption (1 Cor. 15:1–9; Acts 4:12), and no hope (1 Tim. 1:1).

The life we live and the work we do must always glorify the Lord Jesus Christ. We should follow the example of John the Baptist, who said, "He [Jesus] must become greater and greater, and I must become less and less" (John 3:30). Our Savior and Lord must be at the beginning of every project, at the heart of every ministry, and glorified at the end of each endeavor; otherwise, what we do will not last.

During His brief public ministry on earth, Jesus revealed Himself as possessing transformational power. The religious leaders who opposed Him were only the comfortable custodians of an aging religious system, and they resented the newness of our Lord's life and teaching. His first miracle was transforming water into wine (John 2:1–12), the ordinary into the exceptional and the scarce into the abundant. He transformed sinners into forgiven disciples and disciples into dynamic servants and leaders. On the day of Pentecost, He sent the Holy Spirit and transformed a group of believers into "one body" of worshippers and witnesses. "This means that anyone who belongs to Christ has become a new person. The old life is gone; a new life has begun" (2 Cor. 5:17).

In each local church, Jesus Christ alone must be preeminent in everything, no matter how many proud people would like to have that position. The preacher must ask, "Where is Christ in my sermon?" The musicians must ask, "Is Jesus Christ the theme of our song, or is it our own talents?" Small group leaders must ask, "Where is Jesus in our fellowship and prayers?" The finance department must ask, "Where are Jesus and His values in our budget?" Jesus Christ must be "first in everything" (Col. 1:18), or as Augustine put it, "Jesus Christ will be Lord of all or he will not be Lord at all."[1]

The Father has determined that each of His children become more like His beloved Son, Jesus Christ (Rom. 8:29), a process theologians call "sanctification." God's people are not to pattern themselves after anyone but the Son of God. This is difficult in a world that promotes Christian celebrity! This is why we read the Scriptures to see Jesus, we pray to become like Jesus, and we accept each circumstance of life as an opportunity to receive His grace and do what Jesus would do. We don't compare ourselves with other people (2 Cor. 10:12) and pride ourselves that we are better than they are (Luke 18:9–14). We measure ourselves only by Jesus Christ (Eph. 4:11–16). The eminent British preacher Charles Haddon Spurgeon said, "I have a great need of Christ; but I have a great Christ for my need."[2]

1. What activities or ministries of Jesus do you find in the three Scripture passages?

2. Who do you imitate (consciously or unconsciously)? Why seek to imitate Jesus?

The Humble Birth of a Great Child

Read Matthew 1:18—2:23

We cannot help seeing the contrast between the transformations described in Genesis 1–2 and those recorded in Matthew 1–2. Genesis shows us transformation on a vast scale, involving galaxies and planets, continents and oceans, while Matthew opens with the genealogy and birth *of a baby! And He is born in the little town of Bethlehem, in the insignificant nation of Israel!* The emphasis here is on smallness; the greatness comes later. The effect is paradoxical. Powerful God was born a mere man; even more, a dependent infant. Some years ago, the engineers in charge of the Big Ben clock in London had to put a halfpenny coin on the pendulum to adjust it and keep it right. "For who has despised the day of small things?" (Zech. 4:10 NASB1995).

Great humility. Jesus humbled Himself when He came to earth as a human being, permanently identifying Himself with the human race (Phil. 2:1–11). He didn't pretend to be human; He *was* human, as well as divine (1 John 1:1–4). By becoming one of us in birth, growth, trials, and even death, He declared that we are important to God. When He was incarnate here on earth, He could serve needy people, and today in heaven in a glorified body, He sympathizes with our needs and helps us at the throne of grace (Heb. 4:14–16). Because He had a human body, He could die for our sins (Heb. 10:3–14). "Be humble, thinking of others as better than [more important than] yourselves" (Phil. 2:3).

Great weakness. The eternal Son of God was weakened and limited from His birth to His resurrection. If He was in Bethany, He was not in Nazareth. He knew weariness, hunger, and thirst (John 4:1–8, 31–33). He had to pray and trust the Father for all His needs, and He experienced poverty (2 Cor. 8:9). Today in His exaltation, He can give us fullness (Eph. 1:23; 4:13) and the strength we need (Eph. 3:16–17; Col. 1:11). We often feel too weak to serve, but this can lead us to strength from the Lord (2 Cor. 12:10). Transformation isn't something we do for God; it's something God does in us and through us, when we are weak enough to let Him do it.

Great sacrifice and service. Jesus came to serve, not to be served, and people came to Him at all times for the help only He could give. The times were not easy when He arrived on the scene and entered into the burdens and sorrows of the people. He cared for people and manifested His love by living for them and dying for them. True service involves sacrifice, even the ultimate sacrifice of laying down our lives for others (John 15:13). But we don't sacrifice and serve just because we love others; we sacrifice and serve *because we love Jesus Christ.* Jesus helped people who never thanked Him or even followed Him, and so should we.

Great patience. Jesus lived and worked in Nazareth until the Father told Him to go to the Jordan and be baptized by John, and that began His public ministry. In Genesis 1–2, God counted the days, and in John 1–2, the days are noted (1:29, 35, 39, 43; 2:1), and in the rest of the book, so are the hours (2:4; 7:6, 8, 30; 8:20; 12:23; 13:1; 17:1). Jesus knew when to work and when to rest because He obeyed His Father's will (9:4; 11:1–10).

We still live a day at a time, and God promised, "Your strength will equal your days" (Deut. 33:25 NIV).

1. Why is the manner of Christ's birth so important for correct belief?

2. In what ways is God currently teaching you lessons on humility?

Day 56

The Destroyer

Read Matthew 2

During Israel's history, Satan had frequently attempted to keep Jesus from being born. At one point, only young Joash survived to carry on the Davidic line, through which Jesus would come into the world (2 Chron. 22:10–12). But now the Savior had been born, and Satan wanted to kill Him, using King Herod the Great as his servant. Each of us is serving either Jesus the builder (Matt. 16:18) or Satan the destroyer (Rev. 9:11), and the tools Satan used in the past, he is still using today.

Pride. Jesus came as a humble baby, but Herod was an arrogant, tyrannical king. When the magi and their entourage arrived in Jerusalem, Herod no doubt thought they had come to honor him. After all, he was "king of the Jews." But when he heard that another king had been born, he declared war. Herod sought to destroy anyone who threatened his authority. The record shows that during his reign he murdered a favorite wife, three sons, a mother-in-law, and a brother-in-law. His son Herod Antipas killed John the Baptist (Mark 6:14–28), and Herod Agrippa killed the apostle James and would have killed Peter (Acts 12:1–5). The abuse of authority is a mark of a destroyer, whether it is a king on a throne or a leader in a local church (3 John 9–10).

Deception. Herod was a shrewd man who knew how to lie, yet Jesus came as "the truth" (John 14:6). Herod was working for Satan, and Satan is a liar (John 8:44). Destroyers often disguise their deception with religion, and

Herod was no exception. He tried to trick the magi by pretending he wanted to worship the newborn king. Whenever lies enter the scene, Satan gets a foothold, and there will be trouble. "You will destroy those who tell lies. The LORD detests murderers and deceivers" (Ps. 5:6). While we should be neither murderers nor deceivers, King Herod was both.

Anger and revenge. When Herod discovered that the magi had outwitted him, he was furious and sent his soldiers to Bethlehem to kill all the boys two years old and under. We don't know how many children were slain, but one was too many. Anger is a form of murder because it often leads to murder (Matt. 5:21–22; Col. 3:8; James 1:19). God protected His Son by having Joseph and Mary take Him to Egypt. We must remind ourselves that Herod was an Edomite, a descendant of Esau, who hated his brother, Jacob, and wanted to kill him (Gen. 27:41). What a contrast Herod is to our Lord, who prayed, "Father, forgive them, for they don't know what they are doing" (Luke 23:34).

Whenever our Lord cannot rule, He overrules and brings about His will in spite of the plans of people (Ps. 33:11). God knew everything that would happen: Jesus's birth in Bethlehem (Mic. 5:2), His flight to Egypt (Hos. 11:1), Joseph and Mary residing in Nazareth (Matt. 2:21–23), and the slaying of the children (Jer. 31:15). When we are obedient to the Lord, we can depend on our Father to work out His will for our good and His glory.

Evil rulers don't last forever, and Herod the Great died. But King Jesus lives and reigns! "For Christ must reign until he humbles all his enemies beneath his feet" (1 Cor. 15:25). When He returns, He will reward His own builders and punish the destroyers who assisted Satan. "Look, I am coming soon, bringing my reward with me to repay all people according to their deeds" (Rev. 22:12).

1. Are there any ways you are experiencing the opposition of Satan and his servants?

2. Are you praying for discernment, to counter the attempts to deceive you?

Jesus's Transformation Toolkit

Read Matthew 3

"It is not great talents God blesses so much as great likeness to Jesus," wrote Robert Murray M'Cheyne to a missionary friend. "A holy minister is an awful weapon in the hand of God."[1]

John the Baptist was indeed an awesome "weapon," chosen by God to prepare the way for Jesus. John was an instrument of transformation at a time when the people of Israel were under the heel of Caesar and had not heard the voice of a prophet for four hundred years. The prophets predicted John's ministry (Isa. 40:3–5; Mal. 3:1; 4:5–6), and Jesus called him the greatest of the prophets (Matt. 11:11). John's ministry reveals to us the tools God gives to those who do His transformative work.

The Word of God (Matt. 3:1–3). Filled with the Holy Spirit from his mother's womb (Luke 1:15), John's preaching was personal and powerful. Not all of us are called to be preachers, but we are appointed to be witnesses, and John pointed the people to Jesus. "Look! The Lamb of God who takes away the sin of the world" (John 1:29). The Word of God magnifies the Son of God, which is why John said, "He must become greater and greater, and I must become less and less" (John 3:30). We cannot transform people and circumstances, but Jesus can. John didn't talk *about* the Word of God; he declared the Word and magnified Jesus Christ.

Prayer (Luke 11:1). For some reason, we don't think of John the Baptist as a great man of prayer, but what he taught his own disciples must have impressed our Lord's disciples. During his years in the wilderness, John must have spent many hours asking God to save the people of Israel and fulfill the promises of 2 Chronicles 7:14. Without prayer, transformers can do nothing.

The axe (Matt. 3:10). Sometimes we must tear down before we can build up (Jer. 1:10). How easy it is for congregations, or even individual believers, to be like the fig tree Jesus cursed, all foliage and no fruit (Matt. 21:18–19). The tree dried up from the roots, so we must first apply the axe there. John was a radical, a word that comes from the Latin *radix*, which means "root." True ministry gets to the root of the matter and doesn't just trim the branches. John applied his axe of truth to the roots of the false teachings of the Pharisees and Sadducees, and so did Jesus.

The winnowing fork (Matt. 3:12). On a high place outside the town, the farmers would use the winnowing fork to throw the grain into the air, and the wind would blow away the chaff, leaving just the grain. How we need the wind of the Spirit to separate the useless chaff from people's lives! God wants the grain brought in and the chaff burned up. Jesus comes seeking fruit, not chaff. We are to let the Spirit and the Word separate the temporary from the eternal. God often uses trials in our lives to blow the chaff away so our fruit might be seen for what it is, either good or bad (Matt. 7:16–20).

Even though we use the same tools, no two Christians are identical—nor should they be. Jesus mingled with the people and welcomed the children, while John was a loner who preferred the wilderness. Jesus ate and drank with all kinds of people and ministered to them at the table, but John was an ascetic in dress and diet (Matt. 11:16–19). Jesus healed people and even raised the dead, but John never did one miracle, yet he led many to believe in Jesus (John 10:40–42). It isn't necessary for us to do "signs and wonders" in order to lead people to Jesus. God hears our prayers, God blesses His Word, and God convicts the human heart. Use the tools, and trust Him with the results.

1. In what ways has God been using the four tools in your life?
2. Are you content to be the person God is shaping you to be?

Day 58

Testing, Tempting, and Transforming

Read Matthew 4:1–11; James 1:12–18

Satan the destroyer doesn't want God's people to be transformers in this world where, during this age, he is ruler (John 12:31; 14:30), and therefore he seeks to lead them astray. God cannot be tempted (James 1:12–18), but Jesus the God-man and the last Adam could be tested (1 Cor. 15:45). Adam in his glory was tempted in a beautiful garden and failed, but Jesus in His weakness was tested in a wilderness and triumphed. Satan tempts us to bring out the worst in us. The Lord tests us to bring out the best in us. If during our testing we listen to Satan, we will turn the test into a temptation and fail. Note the stages in our Lord's testing.

Satan suggested, "The Father doesn't really love You" (Matt. 4:1–4). The Father had just declared that He loved the Son and was pleased with Him (Matt. 3:16–17), but Satan suggested, "If the Father loves You, *why are You hungry?*" The suggestion to us might be, "Why did you lose your job?" or "Why is your child so ill?" Satan suggests that God's children should never experience pain or perplexity. If we do, either we are disobedient or the Father is undependable. But there is an even more insidious suggestion here: "Use Your authority to serve and please Yourself." Jesus never used His divine powers to serve Himself but to glorify God in serving others. By quoting Deuteronomy 8:3, Jesus affirmed that our true food is the Word of God, which reveals the will of God. "My nourishment comes from doing the will of God, who sent me, and from finishing his work" (John 4:34). Paul told the first Christians facing difficulty to depend on "the sword of the Spirit, which is the word of God" (Eph. 6:17).

Satan commanded, "Jump, and see if the Father will care for You" (Matt. 4:5–7). Satan can quote the Bible—here, Psalm 91:11–12—so we must know how to rightly handle the word of truth (2 Tim. 2:15). Almost every false religion claims to be based on the Bible, and you can prove almost anything by isolating texts from contexts. To put ourselves into a dangerous situation and expect God to rescue us is to tempt God, and Deuteronomy 6:16 forbids this. The first temptation attacked our Lord's love for the Father, and this one attacked His faith in the Father's Word. While He ministered here on earth, Jesus lived by faith in the Word of God, trusting His Father to lead, provide, and enable. Note the word *also* in verse 7, for Jesus knew how to compare Scripture with Scripture to ascertain the will of God.

Satan bargained and made a "better offer" (Matt. 4:8–11). Satan had attacked our Lord's love and faith, and now he attacked His hope. Because Jesus obeyed His Father and gave His life on the cross, He will one day rule over every tribe and nation (Pss. 2:8–9; 22:27–28; Rev. 11:15). But Satan offered to give Jesus this honor *without the cross!* God's principle is "first the suffering, then the glory" (Luke 24:26; 1 Pet. 1:11); Satan's policy is "first the glory, and then terrible suffering." Remember how Satan accused Job of serving God only because God blessed him (Job 1–2)? Unfortunately, there are people who follow that empty philosophy. Instead, transformers "fear the LORD [their] God and serve him" (Deut. 6:13).

Christ defeated Satan not only in the wilderness but also on the cross (Col. 2:15) and in His ascension and enthronement in heaven (Eph. 1:19–23). We are on the winning side!

1. Who or what intentionally tries to sabotage your faith in Jesus?

2. Notice the statements of Scripture that Jesus quoted to Satan. What insights do you find into Jesus's relationship with God's Word?

Qualifying the Called

Read Matthew 4:18–25; Luke 5:1–11

After defeating Satan, our Lord began to form a group of disciples who could live with Him, learn from Him, be given authority to serve with Him, and one day provide leadership for the church. We should ask ourselves honestly, "If I had been there, would Jesus have chosen me?"

Am I a believer? When Jesus returned from the wilderness, John pointed Him out to the crowds, and this ultimately led to Peter, Andrew, James, and John meeting Jesus. The next day, Philip and Nathanael joined their ranks (John 1:35–51). There were many people in the crowds that followed Jesus who were not true believers but only spectators watching a celebrity. These six men began as believers, then became disciples, and then became apostles ("those sent with authority"; see Luke 6:12–16), but it all begins with saving faith in Christ.

Am I a worker? In Scripture, God never calls the idle; He only calls those who are hard at work. The two sets of brothers—Peter and Andrew, James and John—returned to Capernaum to continue their fishing business, and it was there that Jesus called them to become full-time disciples. It's possible that seven of the twelve disciples were fishermen (John 21:1–3). If fishermen are to succeed, they must work hard, work together, and know how to obey orders. They must also have the courage to face danger and the perseverance to stay with the job until it's completed. If they fail, they don't quit but get ready to go fishing again (Matt. 4:21–22; Luke 5:5). Hopefully it's obvious that these are actually the characteristics of the faithful follower of Jesus! God calls people who know their calling and stay with it, no matter the cost.

Do I exercise faith? In the Luke 5 narrative, we see Jesus taking steps to prepare the men for His call. First, He borrowed Peter's boat and used it for a pulpit as He taught the crowds on the shore, but the fishermen also heard His Word. That's where our faith comes from (Rom. 10:17)! Then He commanded Peter to go to the deeper water, and this disturbed Peter, who all his life had caught fish at night in the shallow water, not in the daytime in the deeper water. He and his partners obeyed the Lord, and their nets were filled. Transformers need obedient faith, to follow Jesus and do what He commands. For years, the men had caught living fish that died. Now they would catch "dead fish"—lost sinners—*that would live!*

Have I given Jesus my all? The first disciples gave up everything to follow Jesus (Luke 5:11) and were certainly not "me first" disciples (Matt. 8:18–22). At that time, they had no idea what it would cost to live with Jesus and for Jesus, but they would soon find out (Matt. 16:17–28). During the last week of His ministry, Jesus visited the temple and exalted an unlikely person, a poor widow, who gave God "all the living that she had" (Luke 21:4 KJV).

Do I have compassion for others? Large crowds of needy people followed Jesus, whose great compassion moved Him to meet their needs (Matt. 4:23–25). It took time for the apostles to learn compassion. They tried to shield Him from the parents who brought children for His blessing (Mark 10:13–16) and from a mother pleading for help (Matt. 15:21–28), and they wanted to dismiss the hungry crowd following Him (Luke 9:10–17). But they finally learned. "I'll give you what I have," Peter told a lame beggar and then healed the man (Acts 3:6).

One encouragement rises to the top as we ask ourselves these questions: The disciples grew in their faith, dependence, and compassion for others the more they followed Jesus. They weren't called because they were suited for apostleship. They were called so they might be transformed.

1. How do you answer each of the above questions?
2. Which of these questions hits closest to home for you? Reflect today on this question, and ask God to make you new in this area.

Day 60

The Citizens of the Kingdom

Read Matthew 5

The "kingdom of God" is not a geographic region but *the rule of God in this world as He works in and through His obedient people.* You enter God's kingdom by spiritual rebirth when you trust Jesus Christ (John 3:3), and you extend God's kingdom by obeying Christ. The Lord's "constitution" for the citizens of His kingdom is what is known as the Sermon on the Mount (Matt. 5–7). Three factors are involved in successful "kingdom living" in this world.

Character (Matt. 5:1–12). Being born into God's kingdom is a crisis experience, but it leads to a process that changes us to become more like Christ as we produce the fruit of the Spirit (Gal. 5:22–23). "Beatitude" comes from a Latin word meaning "happiness," and true happiness comes from holiness within us and not happenings around us. Because we seek these spiritual blessings, the world thinks we are crazy and persecutes us (vv. 10–12), but that's the way they treated Jesus. The world celebrates pride and not humility, material wealth and not spiritual wealth, sensual pleasure and not spiritual peace, and a life free from trial and opposition. The world's citizens need to be born again and receive a new nature within, which leads us to our second factor.

Influence (Matt. 5:13–16). True Christian character cannot be hidden from the world, and therefore it exerts a powerful influence on the world. Jesus used three images to teach us about personal influence. Salt works quietly and invisibly to prevent decay, to give flavor, and to create thirst. If there were more salt in society, there would be less moral decay and more godly "flavor" to life. It would also make people thirsty for what is real. Instead, we are surrounded by decay in almost every area of life, and there is no evidence things are improving. Light, of course, exposes what is wrong (Eph. 4:17–32), which explains why those walking in darkness hate us. Light helps to show the way. Jesus said that our good works shine like lights that glorify the Father, and they should shine brightest at home. God's people must be like a city on a hill so that everyone can see us, working together to serve and help others as we point the way to Christ.

Freedom (Matt. 5:17–47). If we are to build character and exert godly influence, we must begin in our own hearts to conquer sin, for actions are born from attitudes. Hatred is the moral equivalent of murder, and lust of adultery, fornication, and divorce. If our words must be supported by vows, we have abandoned truth, and if "getting even" and "paying back" motivate us, we have abandoned love. These negative sinful attitudes destroy character and influence and trap us in the ways of the world. "Don't copy the behavior and customs of this world, but let God transform you into a new person by changing the way you think" (Rom. 12:2). If we think like the world, we will live like the world and possibly be condemned with the world (1 Cor. 11:31–32). But if we yield to godly character, we experience the freedom and the fruitfulness of the Spirit, and we will prove our citizenship in His kingdom.

1. A kingdom requires a king. How is your relationship with King Jesus?
2. Which of these characteristics of the kingdom is most exciting for you? In your time of prayer today, ask God for more and thank Him for that!

Day 61

The Secrets of the Kingdom

Read Matthew 6:1–18

God's children are not manufacturers but distributors of what we receive from the Father. "What do you have that God hasn't given you?" asked Paul (1 Cor. 4:7), and John the Baptist said, "No one can receive anything unless God gives it from heaven" (John 3:27). "For apart from me you can do nothing," Jesus told His disciples (John 15:5). *Because we are totally dependent upon the Lord for everything, we must admit our poverty and live by faith.* The first beatitude says, "God blesses those who are poor and realize their need for him, for the Kingdom of Heaven is theirs" (Matt. 5:3). "We are poor, but we give spiritual riches to others" (2 Cor. 6:10). How, then, do poor people like us receive from the Father what we need?

We receive by giving in secret (6:1–4). This is one of the paradoxes of the Christian life. "Give, and you will receive. Your gift will return to you in full—pressed down, shaken together to make room for more, running over, and poured into your lap. The amount you give will determine the amount you get back" (Luke 6:38). But we must be careful not to be like the Pharisees, who advertised their giving to impress people. If praise is the reward we want, then it's the only reward we will receive, because we cannot get our reward twice (Matt. 6:2, 5, 16). To "use God" to inflate our egos and impress our friends is to defile others and rob ourselves. Because the

Pharisees loved the praise of people, they defiled everything they touched (Matt. 23:15, 25–28). God is looking for servants who glorify God, not celebrities who rob God of glory.

We receive by asking in secret (6:5–15). "Whether we like it or not, remember, *asking is the rule of the kingdom*,"[1] said Spurgeon, and even Jesus lived by that rule. No one is blessed by praying with someone whose main goal is letting the listeners know how much Bible they can quote or how rich their vocabulary is. Peter asked simply, "Save me, Lord!" (Matt. 14:30), and Jesus answered his prayer. And what about the repentant tax collector in the temple (Luke 18:9–14)? The Jews had their morning and evening public prayers (Acts 3:1), and Jesus did not forbid group prayer—note the plural pronouns in the Lord's Prayer (Matt. 6:9–15)—but He warned against mindless repetition and speaking to the crowd instead of to the Lord. We are praying, not performing.

We receive by sacrificing in secret (6:16–18). The law of Moses required only one fast, and that was on the annual Day of Atonement (Lev. 23:27), but over the years, other fasts were established to commemorate important events. To fast means to give up something good in order to concentrate on something better, such as prayer and the Lord and His mercies. We don't sacrifice in order to merit His blessing but rather to prepare ourselves to seek His blessing. In today's busy world, it's easy for our hearts to be dulled and weighed down (Luke 21:34–36). In these moments, fasting may help us refocus our hearts and minds on our Lord. We may give up food and drink, sleep, or marital companionship (1 Cor. 7:5–6), but our motive must be right. *We must not advertise our sacrifice for praise or sympathy, nor must we think we are "buying" God's blessing!*

Then, "your Father who sees what is done in secret will reward you" (Matt. 6:4, 6, 18 NASB1995).

1. Prayer that asks nothing accomplishes nothing. Take a moment to review your prayer list, if you have one. If you've never created a prayer list, now's a great time to start!

2. When was the last time you consciously sacrificed for others in secret, knowing your heavenly Father knows all that you are and do?

Day 62

The Postures of the Kingdom

Read Matthew 6:19–34

One clear sign of a maturing Christian is his or her posture toward "things." By themselves, "things" are not sinful, for God made a material world and pronounced it "very good" (Gen. 1:31). If we are to be effective transformers, we must give the Father control over everything we are and everything we have, including the "things" that are normal parts of daily life. We are to put God first and worship Him, use things, and love people, but if we confuse these responsibilities, our lives will become confused and powerless. I suggest you memorize this key verse: "Seek the Kingdom of God above all else, and live righteously, and he will give you every*thing* you need" (Matt. 6:33). If we put the Lord first in our lives, we will experience the blessings we need for every moment of our lives, and our postures will change. Notice the three transformations that take place with our bodies when we acknowledge the Father is the source and owner of our things.

Our hands will be giving and not grasping (vv. 19–21). It's not a sin to save money (2 Cor. 12:14) or to enjoy the many good things God has given us (1 Tim. 6:17), but it is a sin to be covetous and controlled by a passion for wealth (1 Tim. 6:9). To put money and material possessions ahead of God's rule and God's righteousness in our lives is to cheapen His gifts and make idols out of them. We are stewards, not owners, and what we do with our possessions on earth must be controlled by heaven. When we use our possessions to serve God and glorify His name, we invest in the treasures of heaven, where values never diminish and promises never fail.

Our eyes will be directed and not divided or darkened (vv. 22–24). Our eyes have an appetite; John calls it "a craving for everything we see" (1 John 2:16). Have you ever watched little children in a supermarket? They scream for everything they can see! If we seek God first, then we will "set [our] sights on the realities of heaven ... not the things of earth" (Col. 3:1–2). Said simply, we live with eternity's values in view. Outlook determines outcome, but if the things of this world attract and satisfy us, our spiritual vision will become division and eventually darkness. Division is literally "two sights," and we cannot look at two goals at the same time. We cannot serve two masters at the same time. People who are double-minded "are unstable in everything they do" (James 1:8).

Our hearts will be resting, not restless (vv. 25–34). Christians don't like to admit that they worry, but they do. Sometimes they call it "being burdened" or "concerned." If God is first in our hearts and we trust Him, there is no need to worry. At our conception, He gave us life, and when we were born again, He gave us eternal life, so will He not care for us and give us abundant life? The Father knows what we need even before we do, and He is prepared to help us. "How great is the goodness you have stored up for those who fear you" (Ps. 31:19). Worrying about today's work and tomorrow's demands is living like a lost sinner, not a child of the King. Beware lest your possessions possess you, for when you lose your freedom, you will lose your peace. Put Christ first in your life, and He will control your hands, your eyes, and your heart.

1. In what ways is money an "idol"—that is, how does money seek to compete with God?
2. Are you marked by contentment? Is "enough" really enough?

Day 63

The Reflexes of the Kingdom

Read Matthew 7

Self-evaluation and reflection is a wonderful tool by which Christians mature. Even better is when we allow the Lord to help us examine ourselves. "Search me, O God, and know my heart" (Ps. 139:23). This final section in the Sermon on the Mount presents at least four diagnostic questions we should ponder and honestly answer. Note how these questions are both *reflective* and *reflexive*, meaning Jesus always turns the situation back upon us.

Am I fair in the way I treat others (vv. 1–6)? In ministering, we must be careful to respond and not to react. "Spouting off before listening to the facts is both shameful and foolish" describes reacting (Prov. 18:13). "Though good advice lies deep within the heart, a person with understanding will draw it out" describes responding (Prov. 20:5). Christian love means treating others as God treats us, and Christian love is not blind. It functions on the basis of "knowledge and understanding [discernment]" (Phil. 1:9). When we reflect on our own lives, the same standard becomes the ruler by which we are ourselves judged. Before we try to help people who have specks in their eyes, let's deal with the logs in our own eyes. Eye surgery is a delicate procedure and is not for amateurs. We need discernment lest we waste precious spiritual aid and our good intentions be returned to us in evil attacks (v. 6).

Does the Lord answer my prayers (vv. 7–14)? Prayer is an essential tool of change because something happens when God's people have faith and pray

(Acts 4:23–31). Prayer should be balanced: asking to receive God's *wealth*, seeking to find God's *will*, and knocking to open doors to God's *work*. If I am not going to do God's work and God's will, I have no right to ask for God's provision and help. Our loving Father in heaven will never give any answer that will harm us, but let's be sure we are willing to let God do for us what we ask Him to do for others (v. 12). As we walk the narrow road with the smaller crowd (vv. 13–14), there is a price to pay, but God will never let down His faithful children.

Is my life bearing fruit (vv. 15–20)? Counterfeit Christians abound (2 Cor. 11:1–15), and the best test of authenticity is, "What kind of fruit does their ministry produce?" Are their "converts" like Christ or like their leaders? There is in fruit the seed for more fruit, so do their "converts" last and reproduce? Jesus said that true believers "produce lasting fruit" (John 15:16), and we always produce after our kind (Gen. 1:21, 24).

Am I building on a lasting foundation (vv. 21–27)? It's easy to say "Lord! Lord!" but the evidence of salvation is *obedience*. Our Lord's parable isn't referring to the judgment seat of Christ, where our works will be judged (Rom. 14:10; 2 Cor. 5:10), but to the trials of life that test our faith. The Christ of the Word of God is the foundation for our lives and ministries, and if we build on Him, we will not quit when the storms begin to blow. Religious words and works are not always evidences of the new birth, but obeying and praising Jesus and not quitting, even when suffering, indicates that the persons are children of God.

Our attitude toward God's Word should be one of awe and respect and should result in a life of submission to our Lord's authority (vv. 28–29). Let's be both hearers of the Word and doers (James 1:22–25). Life in the "transformation kingdom" is not easy, but it is rewarding with the ultimate reflexive reward; obedience in this life yields blessings now and forevermore.

Take time to ask yourself, and honestly answer, each of the four questions above.

Day 64

The Work of the Kingdom

Read Matthew 10

The record in Matthew 8–9 shows Jesus performing many miracles, including raising a girl from the dead, but the apostles are pretty much in the background. Chapter 9 closes with our Lord commanding the Twelve to pray for more laborers to help reap the harvest, a command each Christian should obey daily. But in chapter 10, Jesus commissioned and sent the Twelve to practice what He had taught them and what they had seen Him do. Christian disciples are more like apprentices than students, for they learn by doing as well as watching and listening. What kind of work did Jesus have for them?

Teamwork (vv. 1–4). The Twelve were a team, obeying the same Master and sharing the same authority, responsibility, and accountability, yet the text lists the names of the apostles *individually*. God sees us as individuals and rewards us as individuals, but we should not and cannot work alone, even if we are solitary servants sent to remote places. As members of the family of God and the body of Christ, we belong to each other, affect each other, and need each other.

God's work (vv. 5–15). The instructions in verses 5–15 apply primarily to the original apostles, but the principles still apply to God's people today. The Lord tells us where we are to serve and how we are to serve. He also reminds us that we are involved in a work of faith and must trust Him for what we need. I have done a good deal of preaching in many parts of the world and am grateful for God's provision and protection. I'm also thankful for the many people who have assisted me along the way. But I confess that we packed what we needed for each trip and usually knew where we would be eating and sleeping. However, we still ministered by faith and trusted the Lord to meet each need. God's work is a work of faith, and we depend on Him.

Difficult work (vv. 16–39). In those days, traveling was neither safe nor easy, and the good news of the kingdom was not a message gladly received by everybody. In this section, our Lord was looking ahead to the time when resistance to the gospel would arouse official government persecution as well as family opposition. Our Lord's ambassadors are often treated just the way He was treated, what Paul called "the fellowship of His sufferings" (Phil. 3:10 NKJV). No matter how much we suffer for the sake of serving Christ, we must not be afraid (vv. 26–31), because the Lord is with us and giving us opportunities to bear witness to others. We must expect opposition, for we are as sheep among wolves and lights in the darkness, exposing what is hidden.

Rewarded work (vv. 40–42). The work may be difficult, but the Lord always rewards His own servants generously. "So let's not get tired of doing what is good. At just the right time we will reap a harvest of blessing if we don't give up" (Gal. 6:9). No ministry is insignificant, not even giving a cup of cold water to somebody, and don't forget God's promise to those who are persecuted (Matt. 5:11–12). There is work to be done today, and the laborers are still few. The fields are larger and riper than ever before, and we have tools of transportation and communication the early church never imagined. Perhaps some of us who are praying for laborers should *become* laborers! The work is hard, but the eternal benefits are marvelous!

1. How are your daily duties and activities part of "kingdom work"?
2. Identify some of the rewards God has given you for your service to Him.

Day 65

The Message of the Kingdom

Read Matthew 13:1–9, 18–23

The transformation of a seed into a beautiful and useful plant is one of the marvels of God's creation, although season after season we tend to take it for granted. Jesus used seeds to picture how God uses His Word to transform people and circumstances.

"The seed is God's word" (Luke 8:11). For the most part, seeds are small and fragile, *but they have great potential because they have life!* "For the word of God is alive and powerful" (Heb. 4:12), and Peter called Scripture "the eternal, living word of God" (1 Pet. 1:23). A seed gets under a foundation or a driveway, begins to germinate, and before long, the concrete begins to crack and out comes a fledgling tree. When the Word of God, whether printed or spoken, enters a prepared heart, the Holy Spirit goes to work and things start to change.

Jesus compares our hearts to soil because seeds and soil go together. God's Word is so constituted that it can work in our hearts. Jesus also points out that not every heart is the same. On the footpath, the soil is hard because many feet have pressed it down, and the seeds cannot enter. Don't permit too many people to "walk" on your heart; be careful what you read and hear. "Guard your heart above all else, for it determines the course of your life" (Prov. 4:23). In Bible times, the people didn't own copies of the Scriptures but heard the Word read and sung at the temple and in the synagogues. Jesus exhorts us to take heed *that* we hear (Matt. 13:8–9), *what* we hear (Mark 4:24), and *how* we hear (Luke

8:18), and you can substitute "read" for "hear." Careless hearing and reading of the Bible can lead to careless thinking and careless living.

Daily we should allow the Spirit to plant God's Word in our hearts. And as we meditate on Scripture and pray, we are "cultivating the soil" and enabling the Lord to produce fruit (Gal. 5:22–23). As we share the Word with others, we long to see fruit appear in their lives because fruit is the evidence of life. "Fruit ... more fruit ... much fruit" is what God is seeking (John 15:1–5 NASB1995). You don't manufacture fruit; it grows out of life.

More than one laborer is involved in producing a harvest. Paul wrote to the believers in Corinth, "I planted the seed in your hearts, and Apollos watered it, but it was God who made it grow. It's not important who does the planting, or who does the watering. What's important is that God makes the seed grow" (1 Cor. 3:6–7). Jesus told His apostles, "You know the saying, 'One plants and another harvests.' And it's true" (John 4:37). There should be no competition in the service of the Lord, for "God will give to each one whatever praise is due" (1 Cor. 4:5).

Wherever we go, the Lord may give us opportunities to plant the seed of the Word in the hearts of others. Jesus met a needy woman in Samaria, cultivated the seed of salvation others had planted, and then planted more. She believed and brought the whole city to meet Him (John 4). We should take every opportunity to receive more seed into our hearts that we might bear much fruit. We are soil to receive seed and also sowers to plant seed. Perhaps the Lord will privilege us to be harvesters and lead people to Jesus. God is the one who makes things grow, but we must be faithful to plant the seed and cultivate it.

1. What good seed of the Word has God planted in your heart this week?

2. Where in your heart might hard soil need breaking up?

3. Into whose heart might you sow the good seed of the Word today?

We Are Seeds

Read Matthew 13:24–30, 36–43

When Jesus explained the parable of the weeds, the apostles must have been shocked to hear Him use the word *world* (v. 38). They had ministered to the Jews in their own land (Matt. 10:5), but it may not have entered their minds that Christ's message would go out to the whole world. In the first parable, the soil represented the human heart, but now Jesus revealed the world as a vast field needing to hear the gospel, and the seed that represented God's Word now represented the people of God. When sinners accept the seed of the Word, they receive life and they themselves become seeds! We are seeds, Jesus is the Lord of the harvest (Matt. 9:38), and He plants us where we can bear fruit for His glory (Matt. 13:37). If a field is neglected, it gradually turns into an ugly vacant lot that doesn't produce fruit but collects rubbish.

Wherever the Lord plants the good seed (His people), the Devil comes to plant counterfeits and seeks to hinder the work of the Spirit. As "the god of this world" (2 Cor. 4:4), Satan is a counterfeiter and plants counterfeit Christians (2 Cor. 11:26) wherever Jesus plants true believers. The first "child of the Devil" was Cain, who killed his brother Abel (Gen. 4; 1 John 3:12). When John the Baptist came, the scribes and Pharisees showed up, and John called them a "brood of snakes" (Matt. 3:7–10). Jesus called them "children of your father the devil" (John 8:44). Paul went to Cyprus to preach, and a false prophet opposed him, whom Paul called a "son of the devil" (Acts

13:10). Paul also warned us against false ministers (2 Cor. 11:12–15), a false gospel (Gal. 1:6–9), and a false righteousness (Rom. 10:2–4). It is often while believers sleep that Satan goes to work and plants his counterfeits, so we must stay alert (Rom. 13:11–14).

As seeds, God's people appear to be small and weak, but God's power can work in and through them to transform the "ugly vacant lot" of our part of the world into a fruitful garden. While we must be alert to Satan's wiles and oppose sin as much as possible, our main job is not to pull up the weeds but to bear fruit where we are planted. If all believers would do that, the counterfeits would be exposed. Whether we are planted in an office, a classroom, a factory, or a crowded neighborhood, the Lord can help us so live and speak that our actions will proclaim the excellencies of Christ.

Sometimes the only way the Lord can scatter His seed is by sending persecution. "A great wave of persecution began that day ... and all the believers except the apostles were scattered through the regions of Judea and Samaria" (Acts 8:1). In the Greek language of the New Testament, the word translated "scattered" describes the sowing of seed. The winds of opposition were scattering the believers and planting them where they could bear fruit. We can be confident amid confusion and chaos that the Lord of the harvest always knows what He is doing. There is coming a harvest of judgment when the counterfeits will be bundled and burned (vv. 30, 40–43). Now is the time for us to surrender to God's will and allow Him to plant us where He wants us so we can reach as many as possible with His good news. We are *planted*, not buried, for we enjoy real life as we experience transforming power to make us new.

1. Where has God "planted" you? Can you see or feel some growth?
2. How does the metaphor of a seed relate to your life?

Transformed before Our Eyes

Read Matthew 17:1–9, 14–20

Peter, James, and John were about to turn a potential life-changing spiritual experience into a mere religious event. Here they were in the presence of Jesus, Moses, and Elijah, each of whom was radiant with God's glory, *and the apostles' eyes were heavy with sleep* (Luke 9:32). For most people, experience is something that happens to us, but in God's transforming power, He uses experience to make things happen *in us and through us to others*. Spiritual experiences aren't reserved for rote religious services. Extraordinary transformation takes place through very ordinary means.

Spiritual experiences begin with obedience. Jesus took Peter, James, and John and led them up a high mountain where He began to pray (Luke 9:28). We don't read that the three men asked questions or wanted to know the agenda. They simply obeyed and Jesus did the rest. We can never expect the Lord to give us enriching spiritual experiences unless we obey His Word and follow Him.

Spiritual experiences center in Christ and the Word. Too many believers try to manufacture spiritual experiences out of sentimental music and stories or excessive physical demonstrations, but the ministry of the Holy Spirit is to glorify Jesus by revealing Him to us in the Scriptures. "This is my dearly loved Son, who brings me great joy," said the Father.

"Listen to him" (Matt. 17:5). The voice and the glory verified the apostles' confession that Jesus is indeed the Son of God. Moses and Elijah were there because you find Jesus in the Law and the Prophets as well as in the New Testament Scriptures. Any experience that is not centered in Christ and founded on the Word of God is not a true Spirit-directed experience. Jesus had previously told the apostles that He would suffer and die in Jerusalem, and Peter had rebuked Him (Matt. 16:21–28). Now Peter discovered that Christ's sufferings would lead to glory, and he emphasized that truth in his first epistle (1 Pet. 1:7, 11, 21; 4:14; 5:10).

Spiritual experiences produce character. Peter wanted to build some temporary booths and stay on the mountain in the glory, *but we cannot "preserve" spiritual experiences except in our character.* Peter recorded this mountaintop experience in 2 Peter 1:12–21 and emphasized Jesus and the Word of God. Even the memory of a special experience may fade or change, but the Word stands forever. In this life, I don't expect to see God's glory radiating from people, nor do I expect to hear God's voice, but I pray that His Spirit will transform me so I can serve Him better.

Spiritual experiences lead to spiritual service to others. Instead of basking in the glory of the past, Jesus led the three apostles down into the valley where Satan was violently attacking a young boy, and He set the lad free. The glory of the kingdom (Matt. 16:28) must be expressed in grace toward those who need Jesus. God's desire is that the whole earth be filled with His glory (Num. 14:21; Hab. 2:14; Ps. 72:19), and it will be when Jesus returns. But we can help spread the glory today, one life at a time, one situation at a time.

The disciples' failure exposes our own misunderstandings of how God uses authentic spiritual experiences to transform us. God's radical process utilizes ordinary means for incredible outcomes. We must stay close to Jesus and His Word, allowing the Spirit to keep focusing our eyes back on Him.

1. Do any of the above experiences describe inauthentic ways you've tried to draw close to Jesus? What does the Transfiguration help you see about those experiences?

2. Which of the above authentic spiritual experiences might God be using to help you become new?

Succeeding and Failing

Read Matthew 19:16–30

Not everybody who came to Jesus went away a transformed person, including the man commonly called "the rich young ruler." He didn't lack for energy, because he ran up to Jesus, nor did he lack respect, because he knelt before the Lord and presented his request. The man was young and had a life ahead of him but no spiritual life within him. He was rich, but still he felt something was missing in his life. He was a ruler, probably in the synagogue, but his religious practices had not given him peace. In spite of these personal assets, he was very weak in his theology, and Jesus tried to help him by focusing on three attributes of God.

The goodness of God. The young man addressed Jesus as "Good Teacher" (Mark 10:17), a title even the rabbis would not accept, for no one is good but the Lord God Almighty. "The LORD is good and does what is right" (Ps. 25:8). "Taste and see that the LORD is good" (Ps. 34:8). "Give thanks to the LORD, for he is good" (Ps. 106:1). Jesus challenged the young man's use of "good," for by calling Jesus "good," the man was affirming that Jesus is God. And if Jesus is God, the man had better obey Him! After all, wouldn't a good man give good counsel?

The righteousness of God. The law cannot save us, and no amount of religious activity can make us right with God (Gal. 2:15–21). The law is a mirror that reveals our sins (James 1:22–25) and a "tutor to bring us to Christ" (Gal. 3:24 NKJV). Jesus held the commandments before the young man, not as the way of salvation (Rom. 3:20) but as proof that he needed God's grace, for there must be conviction before there can be conversion. But when the ruler asked "Which ones?" he made himself a judge of God's law (James 4:11–12) and selected the commandments he wished to obey. The law is like a chain of ten links that keeps us from falling into eternal fire. *If we break but one link, we fall!*

The uniqueness of God. The young man was guilty of breaking both the first and the tenth commandments: "You must not have any other god but me" and "You must not covet" (Ex. 20:3, 17). Wealth was his god, for it determined his values and controlled his decisions, and in God's sight, covetousness is idolatry (Col. 3:5). "No one can serve two masters.... You cannot serve both God and money" (Matt. 6:24 NIV). Nobody was ever saved by selling everything and giving it away, because salvation is a gift we receive, not a reward we earn (Eph. 2:8–9). But by sincerely giving away his wealth, the man would be repenting of his sin of covetousness, and then he could trust only Jesus and be saved (Acts 20:21).

Christ's commands to the man were simple but costly: Go and sell; go and give; come and follow Me (v. 21). The first two commands are repentance, and the last one is faith. But the young man "went away sad" (v. 22). He was still young, rich, and highly esteemed in society, but in God's sight, he was "wretched and miserable and poor and blind and naked" (Rev. 3:17). "Beware! Guard against every kind of greed," said Jesus. "Life is not measured by how much you own" (Luke 12:15). You can "gain the whole world but lose your own soul" (Matt. 16:26). You can succeed at everything in this life but fail in faith, and so fail in everything.

1. How was it that the young ruler valued material possessions over eternal life?

2. Have you ever asked Peter's question in verse 27: "What
   will we get?" What does Jesus's answer indicate about the
   new heart He is creating within us?

Day 69

Acting and Authenticating

Read Matthew 23:1–12

Mahatma Gandhi was asked what he thought was the greatest obstacle to Christian missions in India, and he replied, "Christians."[1] The greatest obstacle to our Lord's ministry in His day was the religion of the scribes and Pharisees, which, unfortunately, infects churches today. Matthew 23 records Christ's indictment against this "show-off" religion of outward obedience that does nothing to change the human heart. Seven times in this sermon, Jesus called the scribes and Pharisees "hypocrites," which means "playactors." He boldly said, "They don't practice what they teach" (v. 3), and accused them of committing three sins.

They were dishonest (vv. 1–3). As defenders of the Mosaic law, the scribes and Pharisees had the official right to teach what Moses taught, but they were commanding people to do what they themselves did not do. They were pretenders, not defenders, for the best way to defend your faith is to live it and serve others (Matt. 5:16). Hypocrisy means promoting a good reputation while cultivating a bad character. The scribes and Pharisees had devious ways of interpreting God's Word so they could make personal gain even from their disobedience. Hypocrites live on substitutes and never experience what is real and life-changing in the faith. They are actors.

They were unloving (v. 4). The Pharisees and scribes taught 613 laws that the people had to obey, so they emphasized negative prohibition rather than positive growth and maturity and service to others. Their religion was a burden, not a blessing; it was a source of pain, not of joy. The religious leaders offered no help to the people wearing this legalistic yoke (Acts 15:10). Jesus said they were "crushing" the people with rules and regulations and never lifting even a finger to ease the burden. Jesus was a shepherd who loved the people, even to the point of dying for them, and He gives us a yoke easy to bear (Matt. 11:28–30). When Christ is in our hearts, we obey because of love and not fear, and we seek only to glorify God.

They were proud (vv. 5–12). "Everything they do is for show," said Jesus (v. 5). They took Deuteronomy 11:18–21 literally and wore, on their foreheads or arms, boxes containing Scripture verses, and they made the boxes extra large so people would see them. For the same reason, they also had extra long tassels on their robes (Num. 15:38–41). But if we must decorate ourselves to convince people we are holy, then we aren't holy. If we must sit in special places so people think we're important, then we aren't important. There is nothing wrong with titles, but if we bask in them and insist on proper recognition, we aren't worth recognizing. (*Rab* means "master"; *rabbi* means "my master"; *rabboni* means "my lord, my master.") To Jesus, the highest honor was not to crack the whip and give orders but to bend the knee and be a servant who takes orders, for God exalts those who serve out of love for Him and others (vv. 11–12).

"No, O people, the LORD has told you what is good, and this is what he requires of you: to do what is right, to love mercy, and to walk humbly with your God" (Mic. 6:8). Authentic children of God are characterized by truth, love, and humility. Those are the transformers who bring freedom to the world, not bondage.

1. Contrast yourself with these religious leaders. What evidence authenticates your discipleship?
2. Here's a question for prayer: Am I an obstacle to someone trusting in Jesus?

Day 70

Robbing and Blinding

Read Matthew 23:13–24

When Jesus was ministering on earth, religious life in Israel was at a low ebb. The scribes and Pharisees not only harmed themselves by believing false doctrines and living hypocritical lives, but by their example and teaching, they also robbed the people of the spiritual blessings the Lord wanted to give them. The common people listened to Jesus, but the religious leaders stood in their way. "Is there a single one of us rulers or Pharisees who believes in him?" they asked the soldiers who failed to arrest Jesus (John 7:48). These leaders thought they were shining examples of godliness, when Jesus classified them as thieves, robbers, and blind guides.

They were barring the door to eternal life (vv. 13–15). "What sorrow awaits you experts in religious law! For you remove the key to knowledge from the people. You don't enter the Kingdom yourselves, and you prevent others from entering" (Luke 11:52). Jesus is the key to the Scriptures (John 5:39–40), and faith in Jesus is the way to eternal life. The leaders defended their man-made religious traditions but were ignorant of the basic message found in their own sacred Scriptures. What was wrong?

They were blind to spiritual truth (vv. 16–22). In order to enter the kingdom of God, a person must first experience the new birth (John 3:1–16). The phrase "blind guides" must have cut deeply and aroused the anger of the leaders as well as the curiosity of the people. Who in his right mind would follow a blind guide? The priorities and values of the scribes and Pharisees were completely confused. The gold was more important than the temple; the sacrifice was more important than the altar on which it lay! The leaders adjusted these values so they could make vows to God on their own terms and not have to keep them. Satan blinds people's eyes (2 Cor. 4:3–4), even people with graduate degrees in "religion." Nicodemus was "a respected Jewish teacher," yet he misunderstood the basic truths about the new birth (John 3:10). I have heard preachers and teachers and have read famous authors who seemed to know nothing about the Word of God, the Son of God, or the new birth.

They were burdened with religious trivia (vv. 23–24). Some things are essential and some are incidental, but the scribes and Pharisees didn't know the difference because they were obsessed with the minutiae of the law. They ignored the foundations of society—justice, mercy, and faith—while they calculated their tithes from selling herbs. Jesus didn't oppose tithing, but He did oppose majoring on minors. The two great commandments are to love the Lord with all we are and have and to love our neighbors as ourselves (Matt. 22:34–40). People are more important than herbs, and the Lord is the most important of all.

Legalism emphasizes trivia and makes people proud and critical as they measure themselves against others. How many prayers did I offer? How many Bible verses did I read? *You cannot measure the spiritual the way you measure the material.*

1. Might Jesus have provoked some laughter among the common people by His words to the religious leaders? Why?
2. Prayerfully read Galatians 5:22–23, and as you do, consider the importance of bearing fruit instead of manufacturing deeds.

Day 71

Whitewashed and Washed White

Read Matthew 23:25–28

"He that sees the beauty of holiness, or true moral good," wrote Jonathan Edwards, "sees the greatest and most important thing in the world."[1] Eight times in the Scriptures we find God's command "Be holy for I am holy," a command that applies to believers today (1 Pet. 1:15–16). We strive to be the type of Christians whose walk with God is so intimate that when you spend time with them, you go away feeling cleaner and stronger. But the scribes and Pharisees were toxic. They didn't sanctify people; they contaminated them. Jesus compared them to dirty dishes and defiling tombs. The concept of "spiritual contamination" introduces three kinds of people.

The unwashed (vv. 25–26). If dirty dishes are washed only on the outside, they are still dirty. We noted earlier that hypocrites are people who promote a good reputation while developing a bad character. The bowl and cup are washed on the outside but left dirty on the inside, "full of greed and wickedness" (Luke 11:39). By practicing daily ceremonial washings, they pleased themselves but not the Lord (Matt. 15:1–9). If we want to live holy lives that honor God, we must deal with the inside, the heart, and pray, "Create in me a clean heart, O God. Renew a loyal spirit within me" (Ps. 51:10). "Guard your heart above all else, for it determines the course of your life" (Prov. 4:23). We must ask God to search us and reveal to us what's wrong with our hearts so we can confess our sins and be washed (Ps. 139:23–24; 1 John 1:9). A clean heart and a clear conscience are necessary if we are to become new.

The whitewashed (vv. 27–28). From childhood, the people of Israel were taught to differentiate between things ceremonially clean and unclean. If they failed to make these distinctions, they were excluded from the fellowship and could not participate in national worship. If they touched a corpse, a grave, or even a human bone, they were defiled for seven days (Num. 19:16). This led to the practice of placing whitewashed flat stones on graves to alert people not to walk on them and become unclean. Jesus said the hypocrites were like those graves: white and clean on the outside but harboring death, decay, and defilement within. Anyone who was in contact with the scribes and Pharisees and believed their false teachings was defiled!

The washed white (Isa. 1:18). Isaiah in his day grieved over the multitude of people who filled the temple, brought their many sacrifices, and seemed to be very religious, yet were a sinful nation "loaded down with a burden of guilt" (v. 4). Like the scribes and Pharisees centuries later, they were actors, going through the motions of worship, but their hearts were not right with the Lord. "'Come now, let's settle this,' says the LORD. 'Though your sins are like scarlet, I will make them as white as snow. Though they are red like crimson, I will make them as white as wool'" (v. 18). This is the Old Testament equivalent of 1 John 1:9: "But if we confess our sins to him, he is faithful and just to forgive us our sins and to cleanse us from all wickedness."

For almost a year, King David whitewashed his sins, but when God convicted him, he prayed, "Wash me clean from my guilt.... Wash me, and I will be whiter than snow" (Ps. 51:2, 7). It's better to be washed white than to be whitewashed.

1. If you had been in the crowd that heard Jesus, would you
   have been attracted to the religious leaders? Why or why
   not?
2. Ask God to search you and reveal to you what's wrong with
   your heart, and confess it.

Day 72

Murderers and Messengers

Read Matthew 23:29–39

Jesus had pictured the scribes and Pharisees as actors, robbers, and contaminators, and He concluded His sermon with the most serious accusation of all—they were murderers. Jesus knows us better than we think we know ourselves. Had the leaders listened to Him, they would have saved their city, the temple, and the nation.

He explained the origin of their sin (vv. 29–33). They were murderers because they were the descendants of murderers, and all of us have the potential in our hearts for murder or any other sin (Matt. 15:19). We are not sinners because we sin; we sin because we are sinners. The ability to sin is a part of our very nature, inherited from our ancestors (Ps. 51:5; Eph. 2:1–3). For centuries, the nation of Israel had been sinning against the Lord and accumulating guilt (Gen. 15:16; 1 Thess. 2:14–16). It would reach its climax with the crucifixion of Christ. The Lord would use the church to give them one more opportunity, and then the Romans would destroy Jerusalem and the temple and scatter the nation. When we hear or read about an especially despicable crime, let's not ask, "How can people do such things?" Let's thank the Father that, by His Spirit, He gives His children the power to overcome sin and live creative, productive lives. Legend has it that John Bradford was watching a gang of prisoners headed for execution when he uttered these famous words: "There but for the grace of God goes John Bradford."[1] Each of us is capable of all kinds of sin, and we must remain broken before the Lord.

He declared the outcome of their sin (vv. 34–36). When Jesus said, "I am sending you," He was declaring Himself to be God, for it is only by the grace of God that Israel escaped judgment time after time. The Lord sent His messengers to His people to warn them and invite them to repent and return, but they would not listen. Starting with the murder of Abel (Gen. 4) and continuing to the murder of Zechariah (2 Chron. 24:15–22), their fathers were guilty of the murders of the godly servants the Lord had sent them. In the Hebrew Bible, 2 Chronicles is the last book; therefore, Jesus laid on their ancestors the guilt of slaying all the martyrs named in their Scriptures! The religious leaders in Jesus's day built monuments to these martyrs and decorated their tombs, as if to say, "We are better people than our ancestors." But they only called attention to the crimes of their ancestors, *and they were already plotting to kill Jesus* (Matt. 12:41; 21:38–39, 46). Stephen would make the same accusation against the nation when they stoned him (Acts 7:51–54). The Lord is long-suffering, but there comes a time when He must judge.

He wept at the opportunities they had wasted (vv. 37–39). The name Jerusalem is generally said to mean "city of peace," but the city is usually associated with trouble and war. The people had seen Jesus's miracles and heard His messages, yet they would not believe in Him. "I would, but you would not." Jesus called the temple "My house" (Matt. 21:13 NASB1995), but now it was "your house" (Matt. 23:38), and it was destined to be destroyed (Matt. 24:1–2). Do we have compassion for the lost? Are we praying for them, including God's chosen people, the Jews? The apostle Paul was willing to go to hell if it would bring the message of salvation to his people (Rom. 9:1–5). Jesus sent them more prophets and messengers, though He knew some would be murdered and beaten (Matt. 23:34). And when Jesus went to the cross, He prayed, "Father, forgive them, for they don't know what they are doing"

(Luke 23:34). Despite the sin, God pursues and, through the wonderful message of Jesus, He offers life from death.

  1. How do you feel in the presence of a person who thinks he or she is perfect? How do you feel in the presence of Jesus?
  2. Why do people refuse to let Jesus gather them to Himself?

Day 73

Preparing for the Cross

Read Matthew 16:28—17:9; Acts 7:54–60; 2 Corinthians 12:1–10

As Jesus made His way to Jerusalem, He began to teach the disciples clearly that He would suffer there, be crucified and buried, and then be raised from the dead the third day (Matt. 16:21). Peter ignored the resurrection promise and openly protested His agenda. Jesus explained to the disciples that He had to suffer before He could enter into His glory (Matt. 16:23–28; see Luke 24:25–26). Years later, Peter would write a letter to the believers in Asia Minor explaining how, in the Christian life, God's grace transforms suffering into glory (1 Pet. 1:7–8, 11, 21; 2:12; 4:12–16; 5:1, 4, 10–11). It's possible to have a suffering body and still experience the shining face of God (Num. 6:24–26)!

Like every victory in the Christian life, we are able to triumph over suffering because Jesus first has fought the battle and won the victory. According to Luke 9:30–31, the theme of our Lord's conversation with Moses and Elijah was "his exodus from this world, which was about to be fulfilled in Jerusalem." At the first Passover (Ex. 12), the Jews were saved from death by the blood of the lambs and delivered from bondage by the power of God that opened the Red Sea and closed it again. Now the Lamb of God (John 1:29) would go to Jerusalem for His last Passover and by His death save from sin and death all who trust in Him. Jesus was facing suffering and death, *yet He was radiating the glory of God!*

"Because of the joy awaiting him, he endured the cross" (Heb. 12:2). What was that joy? Jude 24 gives us the answer: "To him who is able to keep you from stumbling and to present you before his glorious presence without fault and with great joy" (NIV). *There is glorious joy in the midst of terrible suffering when we anticipate the glory of heaven!* When Jesus presents His Bride at the throne of the Father, there will be joy and glory such as we have never beheld at any wedding. "Yet what we suffer now is nothing compared to the glory he will reveal to us later" (Rom. 8:18).

But there can be glory in our lives *today* as we accept our suffering by faith, receive God's grace, and live or die to honor Him. Paul writes about this miracle in 2 Corinthians 12:1–10, and Luke describes it in the stoning of Stephen (Acts 7:54–60). During the years I served as a pastor, I visited some people in the hospital, not because they needed me but because I needed them. Their rooms and faces were radiant with God's glory—never a word of complaint, always a concern for others, and what prayers! We thank God for all the help we receive from the medical world, but only the grace of God can transform suffering into glory.

There are many ways the world tries to manage the pain of life and provide artificial peace. But the Christian rests in the all-sufficient grace that gives the strength we need (Col. 3:1–4; 1 Pet. 4:12–19). Our task is to glorify God, not to convince others that we are exceptionally strong in ourselves. The way of glory is a cross, and the way of the cross is the glory of God.

1. What have you *learned* from your times of suffering?
2. What have you *gained* from your times of suffering?

Day 74

The Transforming Cross

Read Matthew 27:32–61

If a first-century Roman citizen were to visit our world today, many things would amaze him, but one thing would certainly shock him: the way Christians value the cross and use it to symbolize their faith. An ancient Roman knew the cross only as a shameful and painful means of execution, while Christians today see it as a sign of submission, discipleship, love, and sacrifice. But Jesus did much more than transform the meaning of the cross, for by His death, resurrection, and ascension, His finished work on the cross released the power needed to transform lives today. Several pictures in the Scriptures reveal these transformation miracles to us.

From suffering to joy (John 16:19–22). Many things in life are painful, but in the end, they bring us joy, just as the same baby that gives the mother pain also gives her joy. During the painful delivery, the mother might anticipate the joy to come, and this helps her to keep pushing. This principle cannot be repeated enough: Our Lord anticipated joy when He was suffering on the cross. "Because of the joy awaiting him, he endured the cross, disregarding its shame" (Heb. 12:2). *That joy includes everyone who has ever trusted in Jesus!* "Now all glory to God, who is able to keep you from falling away and will bring you with great joy into his glorious presence without a single fault" (Jude 24).

From death to life (John 3:14; Num. 21:4–9; John 12:23–27). The Israelites complained about the way God was dealing with them, so He sent poisonous snakes among them, and many people died. Then He told Moses to lift up on a pole a brass model of a snake, and all who looked by faith to this snake were given life. Jesus further illustrated this miracle by speaking of seeds planted in the ground. They die, but out of this death come life and fruitfulness. The first miracle is that of salvation, being raised from the deadness of sin (Eph. 2:1–6); the second miracle is the miracle of surrender, letting God "plant" us so we may bear fruit for His glory.

From defeat to victory (Col. 2:15; Rev. 12:11). On that last Passover weekend, everything that happened to Jesus appeared to be a defeat, beginning with His arrest and ending with His crucifixion and burial. One of the men walking to Emmaus expressed the attitude of the apostles and the other believers: "We had hoped he was the Messiah who had come to rescue Israel" (Luke 24:21). But when our Lord yielded up His spirit, He didn't whisper, "I am finished"; He shouted, "It is finished!" (John 19:30). By His death on the cross, Jesus "disarmed the spiritual rulers and authorities. He shamed them publicly by his victory over them on the cross" (Col. 2:15). It is by the blood of the Lamb that we overcome the Devil and his hosts (Rev. 12:11).

From humiliation to praise (Rev. 5). We can't begin to describe what our Lord endured on the cross when, as the Lamb of God, He shed His blood for the sins of the world (John 1:29). But the cross is empty, and the tomb is empty! The Lamb of God is alive and exalted to the very center of attention in heaven. "Then I saw a Lamb that looked as if it had been slaughtered, but it was now standing between the throne and the four living beings and among the twenty-four elders" (Rev. 5:6). On the cross, Jesus faced shame and weakness, but listen to the hymn of praise in heaven! "Worthy is the Lamb who was slaughtered" (Rev. 5:12).

1. Did reading the account of our Lord's crucifixion prompt you to worship Him?
2. Critics speak against Christ and His cross today. What are some helpful responses?

Day 75

Taking Up the Cross

Read Matthew 27:32–33; 10:37–39; John 19:17; Mark 15:21

In the Christian vocabulary, "the cross" refers to *the full and finished work of Christ in His sufferings and death at Calvary.* All that is involved in the Christian's salvation was accomplished by Jesus in that sacrifice. When Paul wrote that he boasted about the cross (Gal. 6:14), he was referring to this glorious work of atonement. We come to the cross as sinners for salvation; we take up the cross as disciples who follow the Lord, whatever the cost. Consider three persons and their crosses.

The Savior's cross. As a declaration of his guilt, the victim was made to carry his cross to the place of execution, and this Jesus began to do (John 19:17). He had been up all night, had been beaten and scourged, and apparently He was unable to continue carrying the cross. Scripture doesn't tell us what happened, but it became necessary for the Roman soldiers to exercise their authority and "draft" a man to carry the cross. The gospel writers don't give us vivid, detailed descriptions of our Lord's death; the text simply reads, "There they crucified him" (John 19:18 NIV). But Psalm 22:1–21 gives us a prophetic description of our Lord's suffering. To the Roman soldiers, Jesus was just another criminal being executed for His "crime," although after Jesus died, they confessed, "This man truly was the Son of God" (Matt. 27:54). *Nobody but Jesus could have died on that cross and accomplished what He accomplished.* What He did was finished once and for all and never has to be repeated (Heb. 9:24–28).

Simon's cross. Simon was a Jew from Cyrene who had come to Jerusalem to celebrate Passover. He never expected to be compelled by a Roman soldier to carry a criminal's cross. However, God had arranged this meeting. Jesus had to carry His cross a brief time in order to fulfill the type in Genesis 22 when Isaac carried the wood to the altar. *But Jesus was not guilty!* Therefore, He did not carry the cross all the way to Golgotha. He died because of *our* guilt. Simon might have been greatly embarrassed, but by the time Mark wrote his gospel, Simon and his sons were well-known members of a church in Rome (note the mention of Rufus in Mark 15:21; Rom. 16:13).

The believer's cross. To "carry the cross" means to identify ourselves with Jesus in His obedience to God's will in suffering and sacrifice and to be a faithful disciple. The cross is not some uncomfortable burden that irritates us, such as an allergy or noisy neighbors, because even unsaved people experience irritations. Carrying the cross means paying a price, denying ourselves, and putting Christ first in everything. It's a voluntary choice that we make daily and repeat for a lifetime because we love Christ. When we take up our cross, we gladly accept whatever shame and suffering are involved as we take our stand for Christ. "The apostles left the high council rejoicing that God had counted them worthy to suffer disgrace for the name of Jesus" (Acts 5:41). Paul called this experience "the fellowship of His sufferings" (Phil. 3:10 NASB1995).

"There are no crown-wearers in heaven who were not cross-bearers here below," said Spurgeon.[1] The transforming power of the cross is ours when by faith we take it up daily and let the Lord work in us and through us for His glory.

1. How do you *feel* about the call to take up your cross for Jesus?
2. What have you *decided* about taking up your cross?

Day 76

Nailed to the Cross

Read Matthew 27:34–37; Psalm 22:1–21

Joseph, the husband of Mary, was a carpenter (Matt. 13:55), and it's likely that Jesus spent His early life in the carpenter shop, first as a child at play and then as an apprentice learning the trade (Mark 6:3). He lived a carpenter's life, and He died a carpenter's death, for the Roman soldiers nailed Him to a wooden cross. When I consider this combination of the cross and the carpenter, three words come to mind.

Indignation (Matt. 13:53–58). When Jesus made His last visit to His hometown of Nazareth, He taught in their synagogue on the Sabbath and astonished the people with His wisdom. They had also heard about His wonderful works, and this amazed them even more. "How could these things be?" was the question on everyone's lips. After all, they had watched Jesus grow up, and He was "just a carpenter" (Mark 6:3). Because they thought they knew Him, they couldn't believe in Him and therefore He could do no wonderful works among them. In fact, they were so offended by His message that they tried to kill Him (Luke 4:28–29).

Intercession (Luke 23:33–34; Isa. 53:12). While Jesus was being nailed to the cross, He was praying for His enemies: "Father, forgive them, for they don't know what they are doing" (Luke 23:34). He was practicing what He preached: "But I say, love your enemies! Pray for those who persecute you" (Matt. 5:44). Isaiah's prophecy of Messiah's crucifixion ends with "He bore the sins of many and interceded for rebels" (53:12). When the Jews were stoning him to death, Stephen followed our Lord's example and prayed, "Lord, don't charge them with this sin" (Acts 7:60). The Romans nailed Jesus to the cross, but Jesus "canceled the record of the charges against us and took it away by nailing it to the cross" (Col. 2:14). All of us had an IOU of what we owed God but could not pay, and Jesus paid the debt for us.

Identification (John 20:20–29). Jesus appeared to ten of the apostles on that resurrection Sunday evening and identified Himself by showing them His pierced hands and side (Ps. 22:16). Thomas wasn't there, so the Lord came back a week later and showed him the evidence, and he confessed, "My Lord and my God!" Though they were able to touch His body and see Him eat, they knew His resurrection body was different because, though the door was locked, He was able to come into the room and leave again without unlocking it. Please note that Jesus had *wounds* and not *scars* on His glorified body and that we will see these wounds when we see Jesus and receive our glorified bodies (1 John 3:1–3). When Jesus returns, the people of Israel will recognize Him because of His wounds (Rev. 1:7; Zech. 12:10), and a cleansing fountain will be opened to wash away their sins (Zech. 13:1). By His wounds they will know Him, and by His wounds they will be healed of their sins (Isa. 53:5).

"My old self has been crucified with Christ," wrote Paul (Gal. 2:20). "For I bear on my body the scars that show I belong to Jesus" (Gal. 6:17). Not only did Christ die *for* us, but we died *with* Christ (Rom. 6) and share His resurrection power. We have the power to be changed—and to change!

1. Which of these three main words about the cross of Jesus is most surprising to you?
2. Revisit the passages, and see if you can find how the words of Psalm 22:1–21 are specifically fulfilled in Mark 15.

Day 77

"Come Down from the Cross!"

Read Matthew 27:39–44

Serving God and others as transformers involves paying a price. Jesus described it this way: "If any of you wants to be my follower, you must give up your own way, take up your cross, and follow me" (Matt. 16:24). But the consideration of Jesus hanging on the cross elicits different responses from different people, and our response must be the right one.

The spectators were insolent. King David said this would happen: "Everyone who sees me mocks me. They sneer and shake their heads, saying, 'Is this the one who relies on the LORD? Then let the LORD save him! If the LORD loves him so much, let the LORD rescue him" (Ps. 22:7–8). The prophet Isaiah also described the scene: "He was despised and rejected—a man of sorrows, acquainted with deepest grief. We turned our backs on him and looked the other way. He was despised, and we did not care" (53:3). This insolence was encouraged by the religious leaders, who should have known better. They were supposed to know the Scriptures and teach them to the people, but they failed on both counts. At the time Jesus yielded up His spirit, the Passover lambs would be slain, but neither the leaders nor the people would see the connection.

Mary was silent (John 19:25–27). The soldiers had pierced our Lord's body with nails, but Mary's heart was being pierced with a sword, just as old

Simeon predicted (Luke 2:35). Mary was the only person who could have saved Jesus, for surely the officials would have accepted the witness of the mother, *but she would not lie!* She knew who Jesus was and what He came to do, and therefore she kept silent. Not only was she pained by the suffering and shame of her Son, but she was also grieved by the blindness and ignorance of the Jewish leaders. The promised sword cut deeply into her heart that day, just as it may cut into our hearts.

Jesus was obedient. He Himself had said that the Father could send legions of angels to rescue Him (Matt. 26:53), but that wasn't the plan. "For I have come down from heaven to do the will of God who sent me, not to do my own will" (John 6:38). One word from Him could have silenced the slanderers. "He was oppressed and treated harshly, yet he never said a word. He was led like a lamb to the slaughter. And as a sheep is silent before the shearers, he did not open his mouth" (Isa. 53:7). The apostle Peter wrote that our Lord's conduct is a good example for us to follow today (1 Pet. 2:21–25), for silence can be a mighty witness. Jesus may have been meditating on these words: "I am doing a great work and I cannot come down" (Neh. 6:3 NASB1995).

We should be reverent. In my pastoral ministry, I have been at the bedside of more than one person about to enter eternity, and it is a solemn occasion. If in the hospital, a curtain is drawn around the bed for privacy, there is not much conversation, and we watch the monitor to see when the faint heartbeat will stop. But Jesus died out in the open, where people from every nation could see Him and slander Him! Whenever we participate in the Lord's Supper, let it be a serious time. Why be in a hurry? He took time to die for us; why can't we take time to remember Him? The next time we face temptation, let's mentally visit Calvary and claim the victory that He won for us there. When others hurt us or oppose us, let's hear Jesus pray, "Father, forgive them" (Luke 23:34). Let's live like those who know the life-changing power of the cross.

1. What would the consequences have been for us if Jesus had come down from the cross?
2. Have religious friends ever used Scripture as a weapon against you when you were hurting? Are you guilty of doing that?

Day 78

A Notice on the Cross

Read John 19:1–22

Where a cross hangs in Christian sanctuaries or in pieces of religious art, you will often see the letters *INRI*. They are the abbreviation of the Latin version of the placard Pontius Pilate put on the cross above the head of Jesus: *Iesus Nazarenus Rex Iudaeorum*, "Jesus of Nazareth, king of the Jews." Besides Latin, it was also written in Greek and Hebrew (Aramaic), but what did it mean?

It was a verdict. Every candidate for crucifixion had to carry his own cross to Golgotha as a mark of his guilt, but because Jesus was not guilty, the soldiers drafted Simon of Cyrene to carry it for Him. Going before, a herald carried a whitened board on which the victim's crime was named. The board written for Jesus must have perplexed the spectators because *no crime was mentioned!* Pilate himself had told them what to write on the board, and when the Jewish leaders tried to persuade him to change it, he refused. At least four times, Pilate declared he saw no fault in Jesus and would release Him, and King Herod had also found Him innocent. Though Jesus was "numbered with the transgressors" (Isa. 53:12 NASB1995), He was not guilty of any crime. We are the guilty ones! He is the spotless Lamb of God, who died for us.

It was an irritant. Pilate had no love for the Jewish people, especially their religious leaders, who meddled in his affairs. They wanted Pilate to use Roman crucifixion to kill Jesus, who they said had broken a Jewish law, so Pilate wrote the placard to irritate the leaders even more. He said Jesus was their king who had come from a despised place like Nazareth (John 1:45–46). They were killing their own king! Pilate wrote the declaration in three languages, which must have vexed the scribes and priests very much, *and he named no crime!*

It was a witness. Jesus was crucified between two criminals, both of whom could hear Him pray ("Father, forgive them"), see the title on the cross, and hear the crowds revile Him. Jesus was accessible to both of them, and one of them took advantage of this and prayed for help. How did this man know that Jesus had a kingdom? Pilate's placard told him so! The words Pilate wanted to irritate the Jews illuminated the mind and heart of a criminal and helped to bring him to saving faith. The spectators at Golgotha cried, "He saved others!" This must have been an encouragement to the convicted criminal. "If He saved others, then He can save me!" The man was saved, not by religious ritual or by good works but by the grace of God (Eph. 2:8–9).

It is a key. "We have no king but Caesar!" the crowd shouted at Pilate and in so doing rejected the King God had sent them. This reminds us of a statement found four times in the book of Judges: "In those days there was no king in Israel; everyone did what was right in his own eyes" (17:6; 18:1; 19:1; 21:25 NKJV). We are living today in the book of Judges because there is no King in Israel. This is a key to world history. There can be no peace on earth until the Prince of Peace rules in Israel. Until He returns, people will "do their own thing" and create a world that is spiritually dark, morally decayed, and more and more dangerous.

The first step toward a transformed life is trusting Jesus Christ and being born into the kingdom of God (John 3:1–3). If we "do our own thing," we live like the world and waste our lives. Pilate tried to "wash his hands" of Jesus and lost the opportunity of a lifetime. If we obey our Lord, then He is our King and life is made new beyond death.

1. The name of Jesus is still an irritant today, and perhaps at one time in your life, it irritated you! How do you see this today or in your own past?

2. The two thieves are quite instructive for us! Reflect upon them both and the witness the sign was to them. Which thief's response describes you most?

Day 79

The Power of the Cross

Read Matthew 27:45–54; 2 Corinthians 12:1–10

The transforming Christian life is filled with paradoxes. The way to lead is to serve, and the way to receive is to give. Those who humble themselves are exalted, and those who are hungry and thirsty are satisfied. "He has filled the hungry with good things and sent the rich away with empty hands" (Luke 1:53). The cross of Jesus Christ is itself a paradox. "The message of the cross is foolish to those who are headed for destruction! But we who are being saved know it is the very power of God" (1 Cor. 1:18). What kind of power comes from the cross?

Saving power. "For I am not ashamed of this Good News about Christ. It is the power of God at work, saving everyone who believes" (Rom. 1:16). The common attitude of those in Rome was to look down on Paul for his faith in Jesus. Yet he rejects the notion that he should be ashamed. Rome was the capital of the empire, but Jesus grew up in a small city called Nazareth. Jesus had a few disciples, but Rome had legions of soldiers. Rome had its wealthy and powerful Caesars, but Jesus was a poor unemployed carpenter *who was crucified on a Roman cross!* But His sacrifice on that cross released God's gracious power to forgive lost sinners and make them the children of God.

Living power. "My old self has been crucified with Christ. It is no longer I who live, but Christ lives in me" (Gal. 2:20). When Jesus yielded up His spirit to the Father, a number of miracles occurred, including an earthquake that opened some believers' graves. The corpses came to life, left the graves, and went into the city! This is an illustration of the new lives we have in Christ today (Rom. 6:4). "We are no longer slaves to sin" because of this resurrection life (Rom. 6:6). The Holy Spirit lives in us and empowers us to behave and become more like Christ.

Praying power. Another miracle occurred: the veil of the temple was torn from top to bottom, opening the way into the holy of holies of the sanctuary, where the ark of the covenant resided. Once a year the high priest was allowed to enter there, but now it was open to everybody! "And so, dear brothers and sisters, we can boldly enter heaven's Most Holy Place because of the blood of Jesus. By his death, Jesus opened a new and life-giving way through the curtain into the Most Holy Place" (Heb. 10:19–20). What a privilege we have to come into the presence of the Lord, worship Him, and share our burdens.

Overcoming power. "And they have defeated him [Satan] by the blood of the Lamb" (Rev. 12:11). On the cross, Jesus conquered our three great enemies: the world (John 12:31–32; 16:33), our old nature (Gal. 5:24; Rom. 6:6), and the Devil (Col. 2:15). "No, in all these things we are more than conquerors through him who loved us" (Rom. 8:37 NIV). Paul gave this assurance to the Roman Christians: "The God of peace will soon crush Satan under your feet" (Rom. 16:20). In our Lord's messages to the seven churches in Revelation 2–3, He makes seven promises to the victorious believers, and they apply to us. In His death, resurrection, and ascension, Jesus "has won the victory" (Rev. 5:5), and we overcome by trusting Him.

Mature and wise Christians are not ashamed of the cross or of the Savior who died there, for they know the power of the Christ who died victoriously on that cross. "For whatever is born of God overcomes the world; and this is the victory that has overcome the world—our faith" (1 John 5:4 NASB1995).

1. Imagine the "joyful chaos" of resurrected saints returning to their families in Jerusalem. What must that have been like?
2. When have you experienced the power of the cross?
3. For what do you need the power of the crucified, risen Christ today?

Day 80

The Wisdom of the Cross

Read 1 Corinthians 1:18—2:12

Previously we've examined the paradoxical power of the cross in how Jesus's sacrificial and finished work on the cross unleashed power for new life. There is a second paradox of the cross, which Paul calls "the wisdom of God" (1 Cor. 1:24; see also 2:6–10). How can the death of the God-man reveal the wisdom of God? The death of a high-profile individual can be a divisive issue. While many are divided over the person of Jesus, those who are His disciples understand the wisdom of the cross by what our Lord's death brings together.

God's wisdom unites justice and mercy so that sinners can be saved and the righteousness of God be upheld. Because Jesus took our place on the cross and paid the debt we owed, God can "be just and the justifier of the one who has faith in Jesus" (Rom. 3:26 NASB1995). But His sacrifice involves *identification* as well as substitution, for not only did Christ die for us (Rom. 5), but *we died with Christ*, which is the emphasis in Romans 6. Because we have died to the old life, this unites *forgiveness and obedience* and we are able to live in victory over sin.

The cross also unites love and pain. The world says that if we love people, we will shield them from pain and, generally speaking, this is true. But as every parent, physician, and coach knows, there is also pain that is motivated by love. God loved a lost world so much that He sacrificed His beloved Son to suffer and die for us (John 3:16). God loved Joseph and David so much that He allowed them to experience suffering to prepare them for their lifework. Because of the cross, we never have to question the love of God. A hospital patient I visited said, "I feel that God doesn't love me anymore." I quietly quoted, "But God showed his great love for us by sending Christ to die for us while we were still sinners" (Rom. 5:8), and she smiled and said, "You're right." The cross says to us, "Love and pain united at the cross, and you can overcome."

This leads to a related thought: **the cross unites power and weakness** and transforms our weakness into strength. This was Paul's experience as recorded in 2 Corinthians 12:1–10. We don't know what his "thorn in the flesh" was, but it was so serious that he prayed three times for the Lord to remove it, but the Lord did something greater: He transformed Paul's weakness into strength, just as He did for His own Son on the cross. For six hours, Jesus prayed, spoke seven precious statements, and waited for the right time to yield up His spirit, and He accomplished in His weakness the greatest work God ever did on earth. "My grace is all you need," the Lord told Paul. "My power works best in weakness" (2 Cor. 12:9).

The cross unites shame and glory. There are worldly people in our churches "whose glory is in their shame" (Phil. 3:19 NASB1995), but thank God for the believers who trust God to transform their shame into glory. "The apostles left the high council rejoicing that God had counted them worthy to suffer disgrace for the name of Jesus" (Acts 5:41).

Jesus commanded us to take up our cross and follow Him because the cross reveals both the wisdom and the power of God, and with that wisdom and power, we are able to experience the full life (John 10:10). Hanging on the cross, Jesus looked like a failure, but just the opposite was true: Jesus was and is victorious. The power and wisdom of God are ours in Him if we will surrender and believe (1 Cor. 1:24).

1. The wisdom of God is unlike human wisdom. Which of the above paradoxical unions surprised you?

2. How have you experienced the power of God through surrender and obedience?

Day 81

Boasting in the Cross

Read Galatians 6:11–18

People today have many reasons to boast. We launch ships into outer space, we have photographed and studied our planet, we have developed global economies, and we have invented vaccines for novel viruses. Boasting is no new phenomenon; in Paul's day people would boast about how many new followers they had recruited, just like people might advertise how many social media followers they have today. But Paul's statement to the Galatian church was just as countercultural then as it is now: "I never boast about anything except the cross of our Lord Jesus Christ. Because of that cross, my interest in this world has been crucified, and the world's interest in me has also died" (6:14). If we are ashamed of the cross of Christ, then we are ashamed of Christ and of His gospel. But if we identify with His cross and daily carry our own cross, we receive some wonderful spiritual benefits.

Boasting about the cross establishes our values. "What this world honors is detestable in the sight of God" (Luke 16:15)—things like great wealth, authority, and celebrity. Jesus was poor. He laid aside the independent use of His authority and obeyed only the Father. He was lied about, ridiculed, and deprived of His human rights. The one important thing is doing the will of God, no matter the consequences. We cannot serve two masters, so we must not mix our values (Matt. 6:24).

Boasting about the cross motivates our service. "He died for everyone so that those who receive his new life will no longer live for themselves. Instead, they will live for Christ, who died and was raised for them" (2 Cor. 5:15). Why should we faithfully serve the Lord? Because He was faithful in obeying the Father and dying for us.

Boasting in the cross of Jesus sanctifies our trials. No trials we experience could match the sufferings He endured, so there is no reason for us to complain. If we boast in His cross, then we will have no problem handling our own weaknesses (2 Cor. 11:30). In my study of Christian biography, I have learned that some of God's choicest servants had "thorns in the flesh" as did Paul, and like Paul, they enlisted their pain to help make them more effective in their ministry. What Jesus accomplished during His six hours of suffering on the cross proves to us that our weakness releases God's power and glorifies His name.

The cross of Christ enables us to overcome our sins. It reminds us that we are not only freed from the guilt of sin, but we are also freed from the power of sin. Not only is there no more condemnation, but there is also no more obligation to obey our flesh and practice sin (Rom. 8:1–11). We were identified with Christ in His death, burial, and resurrection, and this means we can "live new lives" (Rom. 6:4). When Jesus raised Lazarus from the dead, He commanded the people to remove his reeking, binding graveclothes and dress him in clean garments (John 11:44). We have new freedom and "fragrance" because of the cross.

Boasting in the cross strengthens our Christian fellowship. Note Paul's words: *"our* Lord Jesus Christ." When Christ and His cross are central in our lives, there can be no competition or comparison of work or workers (1 Cor. 3:21–23). "For you are all one in Christ Jesus" (Gal. 3:28). The cross is a "plus sign," for Jesus brings people together. If "Christ's love compels us" (2 Cor. 5:14 NIV), that same love will connect us and control us so we can work together and walk together for God's glory.

1. What happens to our ego/goals/achievements when we boast in Christ and His cross?

2. How do the cross of Christ and the Christ of the cross make you who and what you are?

Day 82

Enemies of the Cross

Read Philippians 3:12–21; Galatians 2:20–21

When the Jews left Egypt, a "foreign rabble" traveled with them (Num. 11:4), people from Egypt who had been impressed by what the Lord had done. But the fact that they were with the Israelites didn't mean that they were God's covenant people, any more than unconverted church members today are headed for heaven. We have already examined what Jesus said in Matthew 13:24–30 about the wheat and the weeds: wherever you find true believers, you will also find counterfeits. The apostle Paul warned the church in Philippi to watch out for the pretenders, and his instruction helps us learn how to identify them.

They follow the wrong examples (Phil. 3:17–18). Paul had Jesus for his example, and the believers in the churches had Paul for their example (1 Cor. 11:1). Paul had often warned them not to follow the "enemies of the cross of Christ" who did not follow Christ but practiced a form of "freedom" that was contrary to what Jesus and Paul taught. "Free from the law" doesn't mean "free to be lawless."

They face the wrong destiny (Phil. 3:19a). Those who are truly God's people have a glorious destiny! At the coming of Jesus Christ, their bodies will be gloriously transformed and become like the body of Jesus. But the enemies of the cross of Christ "are headed for destruction." They are not converted people who have the witness of the Spirit within (Rom. 8:9).

They serve the wrong master (Phil. 3:19b). "Their god is their appetite," which tells us they live to please the flesh, but those who are saved live in the Spirit and enjoy the blessings of the Spirit (Gal. 5:22–23). The old life has been nailed to the cross (Gal. 5:24), and they have no desire to walk in the flesh (Gal. 5:16). The enemies of the cross obey their old nature and claim they are living in freedom, when actually they are in the worst kind of bondage.

They cherish the wrong values (Phil. 3:19c). These deceivers "brag about shameful things," things of which they ought to be ashamed. They think that dedicated Christians are "old-fashioned" because they separate themselves from the things of the world, and they laugh at them. They call this "legalism" and say they want no part of it. But true believers rejoice in the freedom they have in Christ and will not use their freedom "as an excuse to do evil" (1 Pet. 2:16). The true values of the Christian life are seen in the fruit of the Spirit (Gal. 5:22–23) and our Lord's Beatitudes (Matt. 5:3–12).

They think the wrong thoughts (Phil. 3:19d). Counterfeit Christians "think only about this life here on earth." But "friendship with the world makes you an enemy of God" (James 4:4), and therefore an enemy of the cross, where true Christians died to the world (Gal. 6:14) just as they did to the flesh (Gal. 5:24). True believers set their attention and love on "the realities of heaven" (Col. 3:1–3). Paul reminds us that "our citizenship is in heaven" (Phil. 3:20 NIV), and that's where our hearts, minds, and treasures should be (Matt. 6:19–21). The enemies of the cross think only of this world and ignore the world that is to come.

It's no wonder Paul was weeping as he warned the true believers about the counterfeits in the churches. Are we weeping? Are we good examples? Are we storing up treasures where they belong and serving the right master?

1. Memorize Galatians 2:20.

2. What are the "daily living" implications of the truth that our mortal bodies are part of our salvation (Phil. 3:21)?

3. Have you in any way unknowingly been an enemy of the cross?

Day 83

The Living Christ

Read Matthew 28; Galatians 2:20; Romans 8:31

We have been meditating on the cross of Jesus; now let's meditate on His resurrection. We believe in an *empty cross*, for Jesus died once for all (Heb. 9:27–28; 10:10), and we believe in an *empty tomb*, for Jesus arose from the dead in power and great glory to resurrection life. But we don't believe in *empty lives*, for resurrection power is transformation power. It is the miraculous power of God to bring abundant life!

Jesus lives! The evidence for the resurrection is so overwhelming that an open-minded, fair examination has transformed many intelligent doubters into believers. In the first place, Jesus promised He would be raised. Knowing that He was alive transformed the weak, frightened disciples into powerful, courageous witnesses and energized the church for ministry. We can trust the record of people who were willing to lay down their lives, not for a myth but for a fact of history: "The Lord is risen! The Lord is risen indeed!"

Jesus lives in His people! The old hymn declares, "You ask me how I know He lives? He lives within my heart!"[1] Paul said, "It is no longer I who live, but Christ lives in me" (Gal. 2:20). In His glorified physical body, Jesus reigns in heaven, but by His Holy Spirit, He dwells within each believer and makes His resurrection power available. If we depend on ourselves, we will ultimately fail, but if we admit our weakness and depend on the Spirit, we will ultimately succeed and the Lord will be glorified (Eph. 1:19–23).

Jesus lives for His people! After His resurrection, Jesus ministered to His own people and transformed their sorrow into joy and their fear into confidence. He met with them, instructed them, and commissioned them. After returning to heaven, Jesus sent the Holy Spirit to enable them to serve in His place. When they needed wisdom and strength, they prayed and the Spirit met their needs. How sad that many churches today depend on human talent, entertainment, technology, and clever promotion in their attempts to reach people, when the greatest power in the universe is available (Acts 1:8; 4:23–31). "If God is for us, who can ever be against us?" (Rom. 8:31). God *is* for us, and Scripture records what He can do for us if only we will let Him.

We live for Jesus! Gone is the life I once lived (1 Pet. 4:1–3), and coming is the life I shall live with Him in glory, but now—today—is "the life I now live in the body" (Gal. 2:20 NIV). How long this life will last, only God knows, but we live a day at a time, asking Him to give us all we need for each day. The important thing is that we live *by faith in God and His Word*. Four times in Scripture you find this statement: "The righteous will live by faith" (Rom. 1:17 NIV; see also Hab. 2:4; Gal. 3:11; Heb. 10:38). We are saved by faith (Eph. 2:8–9), but we also *live* by faith. As we live *in* the Word of God and as we step *out* by faith and obey Him, lives and faith are strengthened and the life of Jesus is visible *through* ours!

There may be times when we think our Lord has failed us, but such is not the case. "The apostles testified powerfully to the resurrection of the Lord Jesus, and God's great blessing was upon them all" (Acts 4:33). The lives we now live by God's grace must back up the words we speak about Jesus if people are to believe that He is alive and able to save them also. Jesus is "the resurrection and the life" (John 11:25), and you cannot separate the one from the other.

1. What steps can you take to effectively remind yourself each day that Christ is alive?
2. Recite Galatians 2:20.

Day 84

A Living Hope

Read 1 Peter 1:1–9

People who live without God live without hope (Eph. 2:12), but when they enter God's family by faith, the Lord in His great mercy gives them "new birth into a living hope through the resurrection of Jesus Christ from the dead" (1 Pet. 1:3 NIV). This hope is not "hope so" or wishful thinking. It is a confident and joyful attitude toward the future that produces many benefits in our daily Christian life because we know Jesus will one day return and that our future is in His hands. Christian hope gives us four benefits.

This hope gives us vitality, for it is "a living hope." You don't manufacture hope; you nourish it in your heart by means of the Word of God (Pss. 119:81, 114, 147; 130:5), worship, and faith in the Lord in the experiences of life (Rom. 5:1–5; 2 Thess. 2:16). Joseph in prison (Gen. 41), Israel at the Red Sea (Ex. 14:15–31), and Daniel in the lions' den (Dan. 6) all faced impossible situations, but their faith and hope were in God, and He saved them (1 Pet. 1:21).

Hope opens the future and gives us opportunity (Hos. 2:15). "The Valley of Trouble" is where Achan sinned against the Lord and brought defeat to the Jewish army (Josh. 7). But the Lord's promise to His people centuries later was that He would turn defeat into victory, so they should not lose hope. Hope looks forward and walks into a brighter future through the doors God opens; despair gives up and runs away (Rev. 3:7–8).

We have stability because hope is "a strong and trustworthy anchor for our souls" (Heb. 6:19). The Greek philosopher Epictetus suggested, "Neither should a ship rely on one small anchor, nor should life rest on a single hope."[1] But as Christians, we do rest on a single hope—Jesus Christ (1 Tim. 1:1; Titus 2:13)—because He is the only hope we can fully trust. On water, the boat's anchor goes down, but we are anchored *heavenward*, where Jesus intercedes for us. Neglect Him and you start drifting.

In the battles of life, **hope encourages purity**, for we have "put on ... as a helmet, the hope of salvation" (1 Thess. 5:8 NASB1995). When the Enemy attacks, it's very easy to become discouraged and to compromise, but then we remember the promise of the blessed hope of our Lord's return, and this leads us to victory. "And all who have this eager expectation will keep themselves pure, just as he is pure" (1 John 3:3). "Rejoice in our confident hope. Be patient in trouble, and keep on praying" (Rom. 12:12). Rejoice—be patient—pray! Jesus is coming again! What a hope!

The remarkable thing about the Christian life is that, when we experience trials and attacks, they work *for* us and not *against* us if we trust God and let Him have His way (2 Cor. 4:13–18). The power of God's promises, especially the promises of Christ's resurrection and return, can transform the Devil's weapons into the Holy Spirit's tools to make us better Christians and servants of God. The result of this living hope is a refined life that has been galvanized against the Enemy's attacks and purified by the fire of trials and brings praise, glory, and honor when Jesus Christ returns (1 Pet. 1:7).

Hope is alive, so we have new, transformed life!

1. If hope doesn't imply wishful thinking, use the above aspects of true hope to craft your own definition of "Christian hope."
2. How does this understanding of hope allow you to help a friend or family member who feels hopeless?

The Living Word

Read 1 Peter 1:10–25; Hebrews 4:12

Sharper than the soldier's sword and more effective than the physician's scalpel is the Word of God (remember Genesis 1:1—2:3). The Word of God is *living*; inspired by the Spirit *of life*, it reveals Jesus, who is *the life*. How we relate to the Bible, the inspired Word of God, determines how we relate to Jesus Christ, the incarnate Word of God, and how we relate to Jesus determines what kind of Christians we really are. "The Bible is alive, it speaks to me," said Martin Luther. "It has feet, it runs after me; it has hands, it lays hold on me."[1] Since the Word of God is alive, we have three special privileges as the people of God.

We don't just read the Bible; we lovingly relate to it. We are not pupils coming to a lecture but children to a loving Father and disciples to a caring Master. Reading and meditating on Scripture is more than a duty we fulfill; it's a delight we enjoy. "I rejoice in your word like one who discovers a great treasure" (Ps. 119:162). "But they delight in the law of the LORD, meditating on it day and night" (Ps. 1:2). One of the secrets of Jeremiah's steadfast ministry was his dependence on the Word of God. "When I discovered your words, I devoured them. They are my joy and my heart's delight, for I bear your name" (Jer. 15:16). "I have not departed from his commands," said Job, "but have treasured his words more than daily food" (23:12). Indeed, the Holy Scriptures are the believer's bread (Matt. 4:4), milk (1 Pet. 2:1–3), solid food (Heb. 5:11–14), and honey (Ps. 119:103). How does your appetite for the living Word compare to your enthusiasm for your favorite café or meal?

We don't just read the Bible; we receive it into our hearts. "You accepted what we said as the very word of God—which, of course, it is. And this word continues to work in you who believe" (1 Thess. 2:13). It's possible to accept the Bible intellectually and yet not receive it into our minds and hearts, where it can go to work and transform us as the living Word. Jesus compared the Word of God to seed (Luke 8:11), and seeds must be planted and cultivated if they are to produce a harvest. We should not only grow in knowledge about God but also grow in the grace of God (2 Pet. 3:18). Meditation is to the inner person what digestion is to the body, and it gives to our spiritual life the nutrition it needs. "Let the message about Christ, in all its richness, fill your lives" (Col. 3:16).

We don't just read the Bible; we reveal it through our lives. This is where transformation comes in as the Spirit of God uses the Word of God to make us more like the Son of God. "And the Lord—who is the Spirit—makes us more and more like him [Jesus] as we are changed into his glorious image" (2 Cor. 3:18). We don't change ourselves; the Lord changes us as we spend time in the Word of God, prayer, worship, and Christian fellowship. As we are transformed, the Lord uses us to transform others and the situations we and they are in. "Then they will make the teaching about God our Savior attractive in every way" (Titus 2:10). We become like "new translations" of the Bible that everybody can read (2 Cor. 3:1–3). "Every Bible should be bound in shoe leather" is an insight attributed to D. L. Moody, meaning devotion to the Bible doesn't do us much good unless our devotion results in godly character and our faith is revealed as we walk the paths of life.

1. Over the course of these devotional days, how has your relationship changed with your Bible?

2. How has digging into God's Word helped you become new?

Living Stones

Read 1 Peter 2:1–12; Ephesians 2:19–22

The church God sees is not always the church that the members see. We may think we are rich when God sees us as "wretched and miserable and poor and blind and naked" (Rev. 3:17). Or we may feel we are poor when God says we are rich (Rev. 2:9). If we see the church from God's point of view, it will help us pray and serve more diligently to make the church more what God wants it to be today. Both Peter and Paul describe the church as a temple, a dwelling place of God, and they give us the characteristics of that temple.

A living temple (1 Pet. 2:4–5). Jesus Christ is the living cornerstone of the temple, and God's born-again people are the living stones that make up the temple. God quarried us out of the pit of sin, gave us eternal life, and "cemented" us by grace into this temple where He dwells. When King Solomon built the temple, the large stones were "finished at the quarry" so they would fit into place at the building site (1 Kings 6:7). This is a picture of how God prepares and calls His people to become a part of the living temple. Whether we see it or not, God's living temple is growing day by day as sinners repent and trust Christ. We may not see it happening in our own church, but it is happening in His church somewhere in the world every day. Jesus said, "I will build my church" (Matt. 16:18)—and He is doing it!

A united temple (Eph. 2:21). Paul uses three metaphors to illustrate this unity of believing Jews and Gentiles in the church: a nation, a family, and a temple (Eph. 2:19–22). When we look at the church situation today, too often we see division and competition, but God sees the unity of His people (Eph. 4:1–6). Nations and families may look divided when they are actually united. Jesus prayed that His church might present a united witness to the watching world (John 17:11, 21–23), and we should join in that prayer. If the children of God don't love one another, how can we convince others that God loves them?

A steadfast temple (Eph. 2:20; 1 Pet. 2:4–5). This spiritual temple is built on the foundation of Christ (1 Cor. 3:10–12), which was laid by the apostles and the New Testament prophets, and Jesus Christ is the living cornerstone that unites the walls. The church that my ancestors helped to found and where I grew up is no longer ministering, although the building is still there, but God's church is still on earth, and "all the powers of hell will not conquer it" (Matt. 16:18). The last book in the Bible describes Satan's attempt to destroy God's people, but when it ends, it is Jesus and His people who conquer the Evil One.

A holy temple (Eph. 2:21). Churches and dedicated church leaders are often criticized and even condemned, but the churches go right on as God raises up people to preach the gospel and teach the Word to new generations. Church history shows that the professing church has not always been true to its calling, but there will come a time when it will be presented in heaven as "a glorious church without a spot or wrinkle or any other blemish ... holy and without fault" (Eph. 5:27). He is in the process of taking living stones and transforming them into His holy design. Our challenge is to have eyes to see the church from God's point of view.

1. Would the believers you serve within your local church say that you are a good team player?

2. Does being part of something bigger than yourself motivate you to serve in your church?

3. The day will come when the church is glorious and glorified. Be encouraged by the fact that God isn't just making *you* new but He's making His entire church new!

Day 87

The Living Way

Read Hebrews 10:19–25

In the early years of the church, the Christian life and message were called "the Way" (Acts 19:9, 23) and Christians were referred to as those "who belonged to the Way" (Acts 9:2 NIV) or "the followers of the Way" (Acts 22:4–5). Of course, Jesus is "the way" (John 14:6), and He taught about the two ways: a narrow way that leads into God's kingdom and a broad way that leads to judgment (Matt. 7:13–14). The writer of Hebrews informs us that the Christian way not only leads to life *but is itself new and living*, and that gives us at least four encouragements.

It is a privileged way because it is a new way. It sets aside the old legal way of Moses that ended at the cross when the veil of the temple was torn in two (Matt. 27:51), opening the way into the holy of holies. The high priest was allowed to go behind that veil only once a year to apply the blood of the sacrifice to the mercy seat, and anyone else attempting to do so was killed. All believers today may freely come into the presence of God at the heavenly mercy seat and worship Him, pray, and "find grace to help us when we need it most" (Heb. 4:16). The Christian walk is not a static legal system but a growing, living relationship that brings abundant life!

It is a confident way. The Jews at Mount Sinai had to keep their distance (Ex. 19:21), and even Moses was frightened at the demonstration of God's power and glory (Heb. 12:18–21). But God's people today are invited to draw near *boldly*, which means "with freedom of speech, with confidence" (Heb. 4:16; 10:19). Of course, we don't come to the throne of grace without spiritual preparation or in a careless or flippant manner. The Jewish high priest had to bathe completely and put on holy garments before entering the holy of holies (Lev. 16:3–5), and he also had to offer sacrifices. "Serve the LORD with reverent fear, and rejoice with trembling" (Ps. 2:11).

It is a gracious way. The high priest had to offer sacrifices for himself, his family, and the people of Israel, but the one sacrifice Jesus offered has settled the sin question for all who have been born again. If we have confessed our sins sincerely to the Lord, we can come into His presence unafraid (Heb. 9:11–12; 10:21–22; see Ex. 30:20–21). Because we belong to Christ, God's throne is no longer a throne of judgment; it is a throne of grace, and we can ask Him for what we need. "But he gives us more grace" (James 4:6 NIV).

It is an ongoing way. We are going forward, making progress as we move ahead freely in the Christian life. Whenever the Jewish people faced trials in their wilderness wanderings, they complained to Moses and longed to return to Egypt. But why go back when you can move ahead (Heb. 6:1–3)? A static Christian life is not a happy or fruitful Christian life. We must mature in Christ as we enter into what He has planned for us. We must encourage others and look ahead and not back. If we do, we will mature in faith, hope, and love (Heb. 10:22–24) and bring help to others and glory to the Lord. We will claim our spiritual inheritance in Christ and experience His transformation along this new and life-giving way.

1. Is your Christian "way" one of *want to* or *ought to*?
2. How do you feel when you come to God: like a welcome child or an interruption?

Day 88

Living Sacrifices

Read Romans 12

Dead sacrifices are not the vain efforts of our lives on earth, but rather, they are the martyrs now in heaven and we honor them greatly. Living sacrifices are those who are here on earth undergoing the radical change of Jesus whom the world misses greatly when they get called to heaven. Paul wasn't asking the Roman Christians to do anything he wasn't also willing to do. No, Paul was a living sacrifice, and to another church he wrote, "It is no longer I who live, but Christ lives in me" (Gal. 2:20). Jesus is a living sacrifice and still has the marks of Calvary on His body as He intercedes for us in heaven. We can live for ourselves and waste our lives, or we can live for the Lord and invest our lives. There are four motivations for why we would want to invest our lives outside of ourselves.

A God to glorify. Romans 11 ends, "All glory to him forever!" and the entire letter concludes, "All glory to the only wise God, through Jesus Christ, forever" (16:27). Do you say "amen" to that? Most of the world has exchanged the worship of God for the worship of idols (Rom. 1:25) and therefore has fallen short of God's glory (Rom. 3:23). But true believers "confidently and joyfully look forward to sharing God's glory" (Rom. 5:2) because they are "heirs of God's glory" (Rom. 8:17). The greatest privilege in life is to bring glory to God, seen best as Jesus brought glory to His Father by becoming a sacrifice for us!

A life to present. In Romans 12:1–2, we present to the Lord our bodies, minds, and will—all that we have and all that we are. As an act of faith, we surrender ourselves to Christ, and we renew this commitment each day. Our bodies are "the temple of the Holy Spirit" (1 Cor. 6:19–20) and the tools the Spirit wants to use to accomplish God's work (1 Cor. 6:13). He wants to renew our minds through the Word to know and do God's will so that we become transformers in a world that needs Jesus Christ. "This is truly the way to worship him" (Rom. 12:1). This means, for a living sacrifice, *life itself is an act of worship!* In the camp of Israel, the priests offered a sacrifice each morning and evening, opening and closing the day with worship, but the Spirit enables us to offer ourselves all day and worship the Lord in everything we do.

A church to serve (vv. 3–13). Each of us has natural abilities we were born with and spiritual gifts we received when we were born again, and they must be used to serve others. If we obey the Lord, He will put us where we can do the most good, and our service will blend with the service of others to help strengthen the church and make it grow. Too many Christians "do their own thing" and forget that "a spiritual gift is given to each of us so we can help each other" (1 Cor. 12:7). The key word here is *love* (vv. 9–10).

A difference to make (vv. 14–21). The emphasis here is on how we relate to those outside the church family, and the rule is: Don't pattern your life as everyone else does. Instead, Christians make a difference by being different! "Don't let evil conquer you, but conquer evil by doing good" (v. 21). We don't imitate the world; we imitate Jesus! C. T. Studd famously put it this way: "If Jesus Christ be God and died for me, then no sacrifice can be too great for me to make for him."[1]

1. Are you becoming more mindful of God's glory? What have you learned through our study so far regarding God's glory that has helped you become new?
2. Is "sacrifice" a negative idea to you (*It's going to hurt; I'll avoid it!*) or a positive idea to you (*It's going to hurt; it will strengthen me!*)?

Training Day

Read Acts 1

The physician Luke wrote not only the gospel that bears his name but also the book of Acts, an account of how Jesus's death and resurrection transformed the world through His followers. We are grateful for our modern technology that enables us to communicate, work, and travel with more speed and efficiency, but it is *people* that the Lord uses to bring about the transformations needed in today's world. He wants transformers to work together, and this is where the church comes in. In Acts, you see the members of the early church witnessing together and telling people how Jesus Christ can make them— and all things—new! Acts 1 reveals some of the conditions we must meet if God is to use us as He used them. These conditions train us to be ready to live out the change we have in Christ.

We must have faith in the living Lord (vv. 1–11). We are not building *our* churches; it is Christ who is building *His* church, and we are laborers with Him. He uses our education, skills, gifts, and experience, but we must depend on His power or nothing lasting will be accomplished (v. 8). For the most part, the believers in the early church were common people, and their spiritual leaders were ordinary men who had never attended the rabbinical schools (Acts 4:13). But they were empowered by the Holy Spirit, and this is what made them effective. The greatest power in the universe is the power of

Jesus Christ, and it is available now to God's people (Eph. 1:19–23; 3:20–21). "For apart from me," said Jesus, "you can do nothing" (John 15:5).

We must be in fellowship with Christ and His people (vv. 12–19). Peter had denied the Lord three times, but after the resurrection, the Lord met with Peter, forgave him, and restored him to apostolic leadership (1 Cor. 15:5). Jesus had already commissioned Peter to lead the group (Luke 22:31–32), and the believers were willing to follow. If spiritual leaders are out of fellowship with the Lord, they are no longer spiritual or fit to lead and can do untold damage to the church.

We must obey what the Scriptures command (vv. 20–26). Twelve apostles were needed to bear witness to the twelve tribes of Israel. Jesus had already "opened their minds to understand the Scriptures" (Luke 24:45), so He spoke to Peter from Psalms 69:25 and 109:8 and told him what to do. Putting the right person in any office is a serious matter and involves both prayer and a knowledge of the Scriptures (vv. 24–25; 6:4). Some people think Peter should have waited until God saved Paul, but Paul did not meet the qualifications given in verses 21–22.

We must wait on the Lord. It was forty days from the resurrection of Jesus until His ascension (v. 3), and the believers waited and prayed for ten days more before the Spirit came. Jesus had instructed them to remain in Jerusalem, and they obeyed (Luke 24:49). When you wait on the Lord, you don't waste time; you invest in eternity. During his years with Jesus, Peter had occasionally been impulsive, but now he took time to worship, pray, and wait. One of the marks of spiritual maturity is a patient and trustful spirit, for it is through "faith and patience" that we "inherit what has been promised" (Heb. 6:12 NIV). The only Scripture the early church had was the Old Testament, and Peter may have been meditating on Joel 2:28–32, which is the text he used when he preached at Pentecost (Acts 2:14–21), or perhaps Psalm 16:8–11, another one of his texts (Acts 2:25–28).

Trusting the Lord and fellowshipping with Him, obeying, praying, and waiting are the conditions we must meet if we want to be transformers and make a difference in our world.

1. Which of the conditions above do you find most difficult to embrace? Most exciting?
2. Even seasoned disciples need a training "refresher course." How are you doing with Christ's priority of relationships and people? What about with God's sense of timing?

Day 90

Transformation Day

Read Acts 2:1–13, 42–47

There was nothing wrong with what the church was doing in the upper room (Acts 1), but if they had remained in that mode, everything would have been wrong. I like that word *suddenly* in Acts 2:2 because the Lord often works that way (9:3; 16:26). We typically gather data and call meetings before we act, but God likes to surprise us. The Holy Spirit came upon the believers and transformed Pentecost from a harvest festival into the birthday of the church.

The major change that occurred was that the Spirit moved the believers out of the private upper room and into the public arena, probably the temple. They still praised God and prayed, but there was a new sense of joyful awe among them (vv. 43, 46). They were not yet evangelizing but were praising God in the various languages of the Jews from other nations attending the feast of Pentecost. When Peter preached the gospel to them, he no doubt spoke in Aramaic, a language familiar to his listeners. The sound of the wind, the tongues of fire, and the praise of the Lord in other languages caused a crowd to gather, and this was Peter's opportunity.

Christians are not meant to just assemble week by week and carry on our "religious duties" behind closed doors. We must take the message out to the people and give them an opportunity to trust Jesus Christ. After Peter preached Christ to the crowd, three thousand of them believed and were saved. What a "harvest" at a harvest festival! Not everybody who heard the Word trusted Christ, because some of them were bewildered and others openly ridiculed the believers and called them "drunkards."

But the work had just begun. These three thousand new believers were baptized and assimilated into the fellowship of the church. We must not only be good obstetricians and bring the "babies" into the world, but we must also be effective pediatricians and care for these new believers and help them grow. They were taught the basics of the Christian faith, how to worship and pray, and how to share both their faith and their possessions. They experienced the blessings of fellowship and stewardship, sharing their possessions with others (vv. 44, 46) and daily sharing the gospel with the lost (v. 47). There was an atmosphere of joyful reverence in their meetings (vv. 43, 46) as they prayed, observed the Lord's Supper (vv. 42, 46), heard the Word taught, and encouraged one another. The believers were united in heart and faith, met in the temple and in private homes, and "all the people had high regard for them" (Acts 5:13).

It was the ministry of the Holy Spirit in the life of each believer that made the difference. I once heard A. W. Tozer say, "If the Holy Spirit was withdrawn from the church today, 95 percent of what we do would go on *and no one would know the difference.*"[1] Let's not confuse crowds for conviction, conversion, and communion. Instead, let's ask the Spirit to distinguish us from the world in the way that makes outsiders sit up and take notice.

1. What are the four basic practices Christians are to devote themselves to (v. 42)? Are you faithfully practicing them?

2. Looking at the first phrase of verse 42, how are Christians to pursue these practices? Using this description, are you living in harmony with God's people?

Day 91

A Transformed Sermon

Read Acts 2:14–41

Peter was God's appointed leader for the early church. He had already led them in selecting a new apostle to replace Judas. Backed by ten days of special prayer and filled with the Holy Spirit, Peter was prepared to speak to a large crowd of people celebrating Pentecost. Because he was yielded to the Spirit, he had the courage to speak, the wisdom to know what Scriptures to use, and the desire to exalt Jesus Christ and bring people to conviction and conversion. May all our ministry of the Word be like that!

Effective preaching begins right where the people are, so he opened by silencing their accusation that he and his fellow Christians were drunk. Having settled that, he announced the glorious news that the Holy Spirit had come to God's people (vv. 17–21)! Jesus had promised and the prophet Joel had prophesied that the Spirit would come (John 14:15–26; 15:26–27; 16:12–15; Joel 2:28–32), and He was there! If Jesus sent the Spirit, then Jesus must be alive. Furthermore, the fact that Jesus is the Son of God makes it impossible for Him to be imprisoned by death, "for death could not keep him in its grip" (vv. 22–24). Peter reminded them that the Jewish leaders had conspired with the Gentiles to kill Jesus (v. 23), so the people listening to Peter were guilty of murdering their Messiah!

But the Spirit added more to Peter's message. David, Israel's greatest king, wrote centuries before that God would not allow His Son's body to decay or His spirit to remain in the realm of the dead (vv. 25–28; Ps. 16:10). Peter and his fellow apostles had visited the empty tomb, seen the graveclothes that looked like an empty cocoon, and even seen the risen Christ Himself and spoken with Him! "God raised Jesus from the dead, and we are all witnesses of this" (v. 32).

But if Jesus is not in the tomb, where is He? He is on the throne! Here Peter quoted Psalm 110:1: "The LORD said to my Lord, 'Sit in the place of honor at my right hand until I humble your enemies, making them a footstool under your feet.'" Then Peter announced the verdict: "So let everyone in Israel know for certain that God has made this Jesus, whom you crucified, to be both Lord and Messiah" (vv. 34–36). The whole world stands guilty before the Lord!

But because of the death, resurrection, and enthronement of Jesus, *sinners can be saved!* "But everyone who calls on the name of the LORD will be saved" (v. 21). Peter told the convicted people to repent of their sins and turn to God, believing in Jesus Christ for the forgiveness of their sins. Then they too would receive the gift of the Holy Spirit (v. 38).

Peter, the fisher of men, cast out the net and caught three thousand fish! During his days as a professional fisherman, Peter would catch living fish and they would die, but from now on, he would catch dead fish *and they would come alive!* What a privilege it is to walk by faith, yielded to the Spirit, sharing in Christ's life, bearing witness to His resurrection, and leading lost people out of death and into eternal life!

1. Peter preached a New Testament sermon but relied on Old Testament Scripture. What does this tell you about the usefulness of the Old Testament and its importance in sharing the gospel?
2. Look at Peter's descriptions of our Lord Jesus in verses 22–36. In what ways do these descriptions exalt Jesus in your heart?

Day 92

A Transformed Beggar

Read Acts 3

Acts is more formally known as the Acts of the Apostles, and the focus shifts from the community of believers in the first two chapters to the ministry of two apostles. Individuals count in the church, and each person can be used of God to help others. We often say, "The church did this," but it is individuals in the church who work together to accomplish God's will. Never underestimate the importance of one believer with one talent, and never underestimate the necessity of two.

Partners (vv. 1–2). At least fifteen times in the New Testament we find the names of Peter and John linked. Before Jesus called them, they had been partners in the fishing business (Luke 5:8–10). Jesus instructed Peter and John to arrange for His last Passover feast (Luke 22:8), and Peter and John ran to see Christ's tomb on resurrection morning (John 20:3–4). Later, the two men would go to Samaria, where they established the new believers (Acts 8:14). John was poetical and Peter practical, but in the Spirit of Christ, they walked and worked together. Jesus had sent His disciples out two by two (Mark 6:7), and Ecclesiastes 4:9 says, "Two people are better off than one, for they can help each other succeed," so don't try to do it all alone. Paul wrote that the entire way of Jesus is summarized in this law: "Share each other's burdens" (Gal. 6:2). We need each other!

Transformers (vv. 3–11). The timing was perfect. As Peter and John arrived at the temple, the cripple was brought to the Beautiful Gate by sympathetic friends. Transformers have eyes to see the opportunities God gives them. Unlike their experience with another beggar (John 9:1–7), Peter and John didn't turn this needy man into a theological case study. He was a human being with needs, and God enabled them to meet those needs. Transformers have eyes to see, hearts to care, hands to help, and voices to share the gospel. They could depend on the powerful name of Jesus (3:6, 16; 4:10, 12, 17–18, 30). Transformers are "poor, but ... give spiritual riches to others" (2 Cor. 6:10). No amount of money could have healed that man!

Proclaimers (vv. 12–26). A large crowd beheld the miracle and gathered in Solomon's Colonnade, where Peter was ready to address them with the gospel. His emphasis was on Jesus, and he used a number of our Lord's names and titles, including "his servant Jesus" (v. 13), "this holy, righteous one" (v. 14), "the author of life" (v. 15), and the "Messiah" (vv. 18, 20). He told them that Jesus was the Prophet Moses wrote about (vv. 22–23; Deut. 18:15–20) and that they were guilty of crucifying their Messiah (vv. 13–15). But Peter and John were also "witnesses" of the resurrection and the good news that the living Christ is ready to save all who will repent of their sins and believe in Him (vv. 15, 26). More than two thousand people trusted Christ (Acts 4:4)!

Whenever God's servants have an opportunity to proclaim the truth and win the lost, the Enemy will oppose and attack, often using religious people to oppose the work (Acts 4:1–4). But the same powerful name of Jesus that transformed the beggar protected Peter and John and enabled them to declare the gospel and defend their ministry. This was the beginning of the persecution Jesus talked about in the upper room, for persecution and transformation go together (John 15:18–27; 16:31–33). When you face opposition in the midst of opportunities, take heart! Jesus has overcome the world!

1. When Peter and John encountered the lame beggar, what do you think they saw?
2. Pray that the Holy Spirit will train you to see below the surface and to see opportunities.

A Transformed Community

Read Acts 4:1–35

Peter and John never arrived at the temple prayer service. They saw the needy beggar at the temple gate and healed him in the name of Jesus. Then Peter preached the gospel to the large crowd that gathered, and more than two thousand people were saved. But this kind of unauthorized religious activity was prohibited by the Jewish religious leaders. As far as they were concerned, Jesus of Nazareth was dead and His body had been stolen from the tomb to make it look as though He had risen from the dead (Matt. 28:11–15).

Defenders (vv. 1–22). The key issue was, "By what power, or in whose name, have you done this?" (v. 7). The council had authority to persecute the church, but they did not have God's authority or power to heal the lame beggar. The temple was a place for people with disabilities to beg but not to become new. The withering Jewish religious system was being embarrassed by two former fishermen who possessed authority and power in the name of Jesus. There stood the healed beggar, and nobody could deny that a great miracle had occurred. The religious leaders were God's "builders," but they had rejected the stone, Jesus Christ, their own Messiah (v. 11; see Ps. 118:22; Isa. 28:16). Empowered by the Spirit, Peter and John boldly proclaimed the gospel to these religious leaders who, in their spiritual blindness, were unable to explain what happened but who wanted to keep it from happening again. The apostles made it clear that they would obey

God and not the council. Their gospel defense made an eternal difference for households and generations.

Worshippers (vv. 23–31). Returning to the church fellowship, Peter and John reported what the Lord had done, and the believers united in prayer. *Prayer and spiritual power go together.* Many churches today have real estate, crowds, money, and prestige, but they don't have power because they don't take time to pray. The church in the book of Acts was a praying church that demonstrated the power of God. They prayed to a "Sovereign Lord" (v. 24), and they trusted the Word of God (vv. 25–26; Ps. 2:1–2). They didn't ask God to remove the Jewish leaders or even to stop the persecution. They only asked the Lord to enable them to honor the name of Jesus by being faithful witnesses of Christ's resurrection. God responded by shaking the place where they were assembled, a sign that He was in control and they had nothing to fear, so they continued to witness with boldness.

Givers (vv. 32–35). As the number of believers increased, it was necessary to care for them, for some had come from afar to attend the feast and needed places to live, and the poorer people needed daily food. People even sold their houses to meet these needs, but nobody complained, and ministering to the needy did not take the place of daily witnessing for the Lord. Ministry in the early church was not a once-a-week activity but a daily delight as the people prayed together, studied the Word, gave, and witnessed. All of this was accomplished by the Holy Spirit working in the lives of the believers. They were a united people, a witnessing people, and a generous people, just the kind of churches we need today and just the kind of transformation our communities need too.

1. What responses do the apostles model for us when we need to defend the faith?
2. What aspects of the Jerusalem church could the church today learn from and emulate?

Day 94

A Transformed Discouragement

Read Acts 4:36—5:11; 13:1–13; 15:36–39; 2 Timothy 4:11

Joseph was his given name, but his godly life and ministry earned him the nickname "Barnabas, son of encouragement." Barnabas's unique ability was his gift of encouragement. Every follower of Jesus needs people whom God can use to change discouragement into encouragement, for discouraged believers will soon become defeated believers and possibly end up disgraced believers. No matter what our given name is, our nickname should be "Barnabas, the encourager."

There are different ways to encourage God's people and God's work. Our introduction to Barnabas shows him selling property and giving the money to the apostles in Jerusalem (Acts 4:36–37). While giving money must never be a substitute for giving ourselves in service, the proper use of wealth is a mark of Christian discipleship. Jesus said, "Wherever your treasure is, there the desires of your heart will also be" (Matt. 6:21).

The next time we meet Barnabas, he is introducing Paul to the church leaders in Jerusalem (Acts 9:26–30). Barnabas was what I call a "hinge person" because he helped to open doors for others. Paul "went all around Jerusalem" with the apostles and no doubt learned a great deal about the ministry of Jesus. No matter how experienced we are in the faith, there is always more for us to learn. When persecution drove some believers from Jerusalem to Antioch, a thriving church was founded there, and the elders sent Barnabas to make sure they were doing God's work in God's way (Acts 11:19–24).

Barnabas was so blessed by the life of the church at Antioch that he went to Tarsus and enlisted Paul to return with him to Antioch to minister, since both were prophets and teachers (Acts 11:25–26; 13:1). Note that Barnabas is named first and Paul last. That would change when the Lord called both of them through a much bigger door to carry the gospel to the Roman Empire and Paul became leader of the team (Acts 13:13–14). They took with them young John Mark (often referred to as Mark), who was part of the Jerusalem church (Acts 12:12; 13:1–5), and Barnabas would teach Paul the importance of mentoring younger believers.

But Mark disappointed them at Perga and for some reason went back to Jerusalem (Acts 13:13). Later, when Paul wanted Barnabas to accompany him on a second missionary journey, the two men had such a sharp disagreement about Mark that they parted company. Paul took Silas and retraced the first journey while Barnabas took his cousin Mark (Col. 4:10) and returned to his home country, Cyprus (Acts 15:36–41). Why did the men disagree? Probably because Paul was asking, "What can a failure like John Mark do for the work?" while Barnabas was asking, "What can the work do for John Mark so he won't fail again?" Thanks to the encouragement of Barnabas, Mark was restored and Paul admitted it (2 Tim. 4:11), and it was Mark who wrote the gospel that bears his name.

Perhaps the life verse of Barnabas is found best expressed in Hebrews: "Let us think of ways to motivate one another to acts of love and good works. And ... encourage one another" (10:24–25). Encouragement transforms even the ways we believers disagree. Barnabas and Paul are a wonderful picture of what happens when we continue to serve and learn and stick it out—ultimately we will agree to the glory of God and the enlistment of godly workers!

1. What are a few "truths about relationships" that we can learn from Barnabas, Paul, and Mark's experiences?

2. There are a million ways to be a Barnabas to your friends today. Pick one or two to encourage now!

Day 95

A Transformed Religion

Read Acts 10; Ephesians 2:11–22

In spite of what some people may say, Jesus never gave the apostle Peter "the keys to heaven." The only way to enter heaven is through faith in Jesus Christ. Our Lord gave Peter "the keys of the Kingdom of Heaven" (Matt. 16:19), which meant he had the privilege of opening the door of faith to the Jews at Pentecost (Acts 2), to the Samaritans (Acts 8:4–17), and to the Gentiles (Acts 10–11). Those of us who are Gentiles can thank the Lord that Acts 10 is in the Bible. Today, God wants His people to witness and to open the door of faith to lost people everywhere, so let's learn how God wants to do it.

God prepares the sinner (10:1–8). We aren't told what moved Cornelius to abandon Roman mythology for the worship of the one true and living God of the Hebrews, but it was certainly an act of God's grace. God is at work in the hearts of many people who are searching for truth. What we know of Cornelius is admirable, for he prayed regularly and even gave his money to the poor! Yet God was about to transform his noble yet dead religion and give the gift of the Spirit. Cornelius was being readied to hear the glorious good news of salvation through Jesus Christ, and God told him what to do. God may not send an angel, but He knows where to find a witness.

God instructs His servant (10:9–33). I have never seen visions or heard voices as did Peter, but God always directs us if we are willing to obey. God taught Peter that nobody was impure or unclean (v. 28). The wall between Jews and Gentiles had been broken down, and Gentiles did not need to become Jews in order to become Christians (v. 28; Eph. 2:11–18). Later, when this same problem came up again in the Jerusalem church, Peter's experience was part of the evidence that God's saving grace included both Jews and Gentiles (Acts 15:6–11). If our hearts are open to the Spirit, He will teach us and guide us through the Word.

God uses His Word (10:34–48). Peter preached Christ to the group Cornelius had gathered and told them that "everyone who believes in him will have their sins forgiven through his name" (v. 43). When they heard that promise, they immediately believed and received the Holy Spirit as evidence that they had been born again. There were now saved Gentiles in the body of Christ along with the Jews and Samaritans, and Peter had used his "keys" to open the doors for them. Paul would take up the evangelization of the Gentiles and, for the rest of his life, defend salvation by the grace of God through faith in Jesus Christ—plus nothing else.

God defends His servant (Acts 11:1–18). From the beginning, there has been in the church a strong and vocal legalistic party, and they are with us today. They insist that sinners are saved by faith in Christ plus good works, including being baptized the "right" way as authorized by the "right" church, obeying dietary laws, and observing special days. Peter was criticized for entering the house of a Gentile, eating with the Gentiles, and sharing the gospel with them. Peter did not argue but let God defend him as he recounted all that had happened. "And since God gave these Gentiles the same gift he gave us when we believed in the Lord Jesus Christ, who was I to stand in God's way?" (v. 17). Peter would not object to God's activity, and the others likewise "stopped objecting" (v. 18). The one thing that usually stands in God's way is the disobedience of God's people who fail to witness to the lost as God gives opportunity.

1. Whom does God include among the "redeemed"? (See Revelation 5:9 NKJV.) When you search your heart, is there anyone, or any group of people, that would make you feel uncomfortable if they trusted Christ?

2. How can we demonstrate grace to a new believer, especially as we recognize the new beginning God is working in him or her?

A Transformed Friendship

Read Acts 18:1–11, 18–28

·

It was Paul's conviction that he could better serve the Lord as a single man, so he never married. But he certainly had a great "family" of friends. In Romans 16, he greets twenty-six of them by name and two more whom he doesn't name, and he mentions others throughout his letters. The friends we make (and who help to make us) are important not only to us but also to the work of the Lord. Eleanor Roosevelt is often quoted as saying, "Many people will walk in and out of your life, but only true friends will leave footprints in your heart." Paul's heart bore many footprints, and he left many footprints behind on the hearts of others.

Two important friends in Paul's circle were Aquila and Priscilla, a Jewish couple who went to Corinth when Claudius Caesar evicted the Jews from Rome. They were successful leatherworkers (or tentmakers), which was also Paul's vocation, for every Jewish rabbi was expected to know a trade. There was a special street in Corinth where the leatherworkers would be found, and that's probably where they met Paul. Their friendship was bound by a threefold cord: all of them were Christians, Jews, and leatherworkers, and at that time Paul needed them very much. "I came to you [the Corinthians] in weakness—timid and trembling" (1 Cor. 2:3).

After eighteen months in Corinth, Paul accompanied his friends to Ephesus and then went on to Jerusalem, promising to come back. While he was gone, Aquila and Priscilla helped to prepare the way for the remarkable ministry Paul had after he returned (Acts 19:8–12). They had a church in their house (1 Cor. 16:19), and they gave private instruction to the gifted Apollos to round out his theology (Acts 18:24–28). When they returned to Rome, Aquila and Priscilla again had a church in their house (Rom. 16:3–5). Paul's greeting reveals that this loyal couple risked their lives to help him, although we don't know the details.

Aquila and Priscilla demonstrated that business, marriage, and ministry can go together to the glory of God, and wherever God placed them, they looked for people to lead to Christ. They worked with Paul in Corinth and in Ephesus, and they eventually went back to Rome. When Paul arrived in Rome as a prisoner, if Aquila and Priscilla were still there, they would have been on hand to welcome him and minister to him (Acts 28:11–15).

Even the greatest leaders cannot accomplish much by themselves. Paul needed Aquila and Priscilla and was grateful to the Lord for them. Their home was a refuge for him, just as Elisha found refuge in a godly home (2 Kings 4:8–37) and Jesus in the home in Bethany (Luke 10:38–42). During some busy years as a pastor, my wife and I had friends who welcomed us into their homes and never told anyone we had been there. What spiritual and social refreshment they brought to us!

Throughout Christian history, "Aquilas and Priscillas" have privately ministered to God's servants. That Paul met this godly couple was providential, not circumstantial, for God knew that they were the "family" Paul needed. Much is made in Scripture of loving hospitality, for it is a ministry that helps God's servants and brings blessing to God's people (Heb. 13:1–2). Despite their low profile in Scripture, they accomplished much to the glory of God.

1. Name the Christian friends who have influenced and encouraged you. Thank them. Pray for them.
2. Seek to encourage the spiritual leaders of your church.
3. Create relational space in your life to forge a new Christian friendship.

Day 97

A Transformed Farewell

Read Acts 20:13–38; Philippians 3:17–19; Romans 9:1–3

Paul's farewell address to the Ephesian church leaders is a moving message in which he reviews his past ministry in Ephesus (Acts 20:18–21), explains his present plans to go to Jerusalem (vv. 22–27), and warns about future dangers facing the church (vv. 28–35). Three times in the passage, you find tears mentioned (vv. 19, 31, 37), for it was a painfully moving occasion for Paul and his dear friends.

We find ourselves weeping as we serve the Lord (v. 19). If your heart is in your ministry, you will find yourself weeping, not because people have hurt you but because they are hurting themselves, the church, and the Lord. After all, Jesus wept and was "a man of sorrows, acquainted with deepest grief" (Isa. 53:3; see also John 11:35; Luke 19:41; Heb. 5:7). God's servants must be like the "weeping prophet," Jeremiah—broken before God but bold before men. Our service produces a harvest if we sow the seed and water it with our tears and prayers (Ps. 126:5–6).

We also weep when we must warn the saints (v. 21). Wherever God's servants faithfully care for the flock, the Enemy will attack and try to scatter and destroy the sheep. The word *Episcopal* comes from a Greek word that means "overseer," because the shepherd must constantly be on guard watching over the flock. Paul warned about false teachers from the outside and troublemakers on the inside (vv. 29–30). Paul wept over the worldly counterfeit Christians in the churches (Phil. 3:17–19), people who live for the world and the flesh but claim to be children of God. "Rivers of tears gush from my eyes because people disobey your instructions" (Ps. 119:136).

Like Paul, **we should also weep over the lost (Rom. 9:1–3).** Jesus wept over the lost people in Jerusalem (Luke 19:41). They had heard His teaching and seen His miracles, and yet they rejected His grace. Paul was willing to go to hell for the salvation of the Jews, following the example of Moses, who made a similar offer to the Lord (Ex. 32:30–35). If praying for the lost doesn't bring tears to our eyes, how can there ever be a witness on our lips?

The scene closes with **Paul and his friends weeping over their parting (Acts 20:37).** This scene was repeated several days later in Caesarea when the believers begged Paul not to go to Jerusalem (Acts 21:10–14). Christians are human and have every right to weep when family members or dear friends leave them. Yes, we know we will be reunited with our saved loved ones in heaven, but we still feel the pain of their absence from our lives. Paul and his Ephesian friends have been together in heaven for centuries now, and one day we shall join them.

So how, exactly, was this farewell transformed? David tells us in Psalm 30: "Weeping may last through the night, but joy comes with the morning.... You have taken away my clothes of mourning and clothed me with joy" (Ps. vv. 5, 11). When we see Jesus, all our sorrows will be transformed into joy and there will be no more pain or death. Our tears, recorded and collected by the Lord (Ps. 56:8), will become jewels for His glory. When Jesus is your Savior and Lord, your tears are not lost nor wasted. They are invested to the eternal glory of the Son of God.

1. What makes you cry? What does that reveal about you?

2. What is the role of "godly emotion" in the Christian life?

3. What "gospel goodbyes" have you endured? In what ways did God use those new seasons of faith to bring Himself glory?

A Transformed Storm

Read Acts 27

This is a long but exciting chapter, and in it we see Paul at his very best. Had Paul not had moments of difficulty and perseverance, we might not believe what he wrote in Romans 8:28, that God had a purpose for it all. Paul didn't ask the Lord to stop the storm, but for two weeks, each new storm crisis revealed in Paul faith and courage that honored the Lord.

Paul the prisoner (Acts 25:11–12). "I must go on to Rome," Paul told the saints in Ephesus (Acts 19:21), and he expressed the same desire when he wrote to the believers in Rome (Rom. 1:10–15). Remaining in Judea would have been dangerous for Paul because the Jewish religious leaders there wanted to kill him. Paul used his privilege as a Roman citizen to ask for a trial before Caesar in Rome, and his request was granted. Paul knew that the Lord was in charge of the whole enterprise, so he had no fear. "Commit everything you do to the LORD. Trust him, and he will help you" (Ps. 37:5). By the grace of God, Paul had already survived three shipwrecks (2 Cor. 11:25), and he saw himself as "a prisoner of Christ Jesus" and "a prisoner for serving the Lord" (Eph. 3:1; 4:1), not as a prisoner of Rome. Who our master is makes a great difference in the way we live.

Paul the believer (Acts 27:10–15, 22–26). Paul was a seasoned traveler who possibly knew more about shipping than anybody else on board. God told Paul that danger lay ahead, but the "experts" ignored his warning. Encouraged by a promising south wind, the pilot steered the ship right into a violent storm. But Jesus had already told Paul that he would minister in Rome (Acts 23:11), and the angel promised him that everybody on board would be spared (Acts 27:23–25). "Take courage!" was Paul's message to them (vv. 22, 25), for faith in God's promises always encourages the heart (v. 36). There were 276 passengers on the ship (v. 37), but except for Paul's associates Luke and Aristarchus, there were likely no other believers among them. It was Paul's faith in the Lord and God's plans for Paul that saved all of them from death!

Paul the leader (vv. 21–26, 31, 33–34). The centurion had learned to trust Paul, who became the man in charge. He had warned them that trouble lay ahead (vv. 9–12), and his words had proved true. He shared with them the good news that God would protect all of them and take them safely to shore (vv. 21–26). Paul swiftly intervened when some of the sailors rejected God's promise and tried to escape from the faltering ship (vv. 30–32). After two weeks of rain, darkness, wind, and waves, Paul encouraged everyone to eat some food (vv. 33–38), and he boldly gave thanks to the Lord for His care and provision. "Then everyone was encouraged" (v. 36).

A storm will bring out either the worst or the best in us. A storm helps to make a person, and it also shows what a person is made of. The disciples had many journeys with Jesus through wind and waves, and it increased their faith and allowed them to reach their destination with Jesus. Amazingly, after three months on Malta, Paul and his group boarded a ship heading for Rome, and Luke recorded these words: "And so we came to Rome" (Acts 28:14). God always has a way of working out His intended purposes, despite the storms.

1. How do Paul's "bedrock beliefs" in this storm inform how we should act in trials?

2. Paul experienced a literal storm at sea. What spiritual storms has God brought you through? How did He work things "for good"?

Day 99

A Transformed Shipwreck

Read Acts 28:1–10

Paul's extensive travels put him in many unique situations uncommon to us. The Italian cruise ship that sank off the coast of Tuscany in recent years brought renewed attention to the dangers of sea travel. But in the aftermath of the event, it was revealed that the odds of dying on a sinking cruise ship today are less than one in six million.[1] While incredibly rare for us today, shipwrecks were commonplace in Paul's day. In fact, we have record of four specific instances of Paul's travels being sidetracked by shipwreck! "Our extremity," said Spurgeon, "is God's opportunity."[2] Paul's apparent reward for pressing on in faithful obedience despite the obstacles was shipwreck on an unfamiliar island. Paul's example on Malta shows us how to keep going when it seems nothing is working.

First, we get busy helping others. Like a common slave, Paul picked up sticks and helped keep the fire going (v. 3). If anyone had reason to do nothing, it was Paul! He was the prisoner to be guarded, yet whatever privileges being the bottom rung on the ladder afforded him, he stooped lower. He took the form of a humble servant. Perhaps these words, which he would write to a church in Philippi about Jesus (Phil. 2:3–7), were being formed in his heart while picking up sticks in the cold rain? We must always remember there are tasks for us to perform that may not be glamorous, but they are important to others and to us if we are seeking to do the will of God.

Second, we look for God's help. From shipwreck to snakebite, no wonder the local people assumed Paul was cursed (v. 4)! But God had already provided from the thicket of wood a way of escape: the fire itself. If you or I were Paul, we might be tempted to feel sorry for ourselves after such a disastrous experience. But Paul saw the hand of God at work helping him along the way. From the Lord's words that Paul would testify in Rome (Acts 23:11) to the numerous ways his life had been preserved, we see that Paul's faith stood on God's promises instead of on circumstances.

Third, we accept help ourselves. From common tasks to the miraculous, Paul healed many people and shared the gospel with them. Paul brought salt and light to the people of the island, and they showed their appreciation by outfitting him and his friends for their trip to Rome. It takes grace to serve others, and it takes grace to receive from others, and Paul knew this and accepted their help. Perhaps this act of kindness was in the back of Paul's mind when he would later write to another helpful community, "And this same God who takes care of me will supply all your needs from his glorious riches, which have been given to us in Christ Jesus" (Phil. 4:19). Paul gladly accepted help, knowing that God works in the giving just as much as in the receiving.

Self-sufficiency is a false virtue for the Christian. Still, many today would rather quietly struggle than receive any help from companions. It takes faith to know God is working in the trials, and faith to let others meet our needs. Paul did both, the helping and the being helped, because he trusted God was working. Out of a shipwreck was forged a new partnership and a renewed mission. Paul's life verifies Jesus's words when He said to "seek first the kingdom of God and His righteousness, and all these things shall be added to you" (Matt. 6:33 NKJV).

1. Are you willing to serve by doing basic, necessary, even invisible tasks?
2. Are you able to receive help from other believers?

Day 100

A Transformed Sentence

Read Acts 28:11–31

"And so we came to Rome" (v. 14).

From ministering to the people of Malta, Paul turned to greeting the Roman Christians who went out to meet him and encourage him (vv. 11–15). We aren't told how the Roman believers discovered that Paul had arrived, but the Lord saw to it that these strangers were there to welcome him and assist him. Even the emperor's officials were cooperative and allowed Paul to rent his own house and use it for ministry. Whether he was on a boat, on an island, on a Roman road, or in his own house, Paul was always thinking of others and blessing them. What a journey for a man who used to arrest and scheme against Christians, who found himself arrested as a Christian!

Paul made the most of his sentence to house arrest. First, he met with the Jewish synagogue leaders and invested an entire day explaining the gospel. "To the Jew first" was Paul's policy (Rom. 1:16 NASB1995; see also 2:9–10), and then he would turn to the Gentiles. It appears that half of the Jewish leaders believed the message and were born again. They took the gospel back to their synagogues, and it's likely that entire synagogues became Christian. The other half rejected Paul's message, fulfilling the words of Isaiah 6:9–10.

It seemed as though Paul was on a dead-end street until he was released two years later, but that wasn't the case at all. The book of Acts begins with the Holy Spirit opening the door of faith to the Jews (Acts 2), the Samaritans

(Acts 8), and the Gentiles (Acts 10), and now it closes with Paul having an open door to anyone who wanted to visit him and hear about Jesus and the kingdom of God. Imagine being the Roman soldiers who were successively chained to Paul each day! As Paul taught the Word, they listened, and some of them were saved. Now there were saints in Caesar's household (Phil. 4:22)!

God's plans and purposes will always be accomplished. He desires that all will "be saved and ... come to the knowledge of the truth" (1 Tim. 2:4 NKJV). Paul's ministry shows us what God will do when a sinner is transformed by the truth of the resurrected Jesus: He will put us on a path to help others come to know Jesus through us. Paul became new when he met Jesus on the road (Acts 9), and he became an instrument of transformation for the sake of the world as he let the truth of the resurrection of Jesus shape his life. "And so we came to Rome" reminds all of us that God will bring us where He promises.

Your situation may seem impossible, but if you magnify Jesus and seek to serve others, the Lord will open doors of opportunity that will transform you and others through you. God's deep desire for your life is that you would become new too. Rome was not the end of Paul's story, though it was the end of his journey as we know it. In Rome, Paul used his time to bring anyone who would listen to the knowledge of the resurrected Jesus. It was in the prison system when Paul wrote to his friends that he had "learned the secret of living in every situation.... I can do everything through Christ, who gives me strength" (Phil. 4:12–13). No matter where you find yourself today reading these words, the Spirit of God is calling you to find a transformed life in Jesus. He's the point of the whole Book.

1. Are you making the most of the circumstances in which God has placed you?
2. Is God proving to you this truth from Paul's life? "My limitations do not limit God."

Afterword

Your one-hundred-day journey through the transforming texts of Scripture I selected has now ended, but I strongly urge you to start another journey. There is so much more for all of us to learn from the Word of God, so don't let a day go by without reading the Word, meditating on it, and asking God to use it to change you and, through you, to change others. As others are changed, their world is also changed. Be a transformer, not a conformer. You may want to go through this book again to "gather up the fragments" that you may have missed the first time. Maybe you skipped some of the related passages the first time. That's okay—dig a little deeper on the next go-round.

We're back to where we started, considering that Greek word in Romans 12:2: *metamorphosis*. Take a moment to reflect over the past one hundred days, and see if you can't trace a line of transformation taking place in your own heart. Have you noticed an attitude change? A new perspective on life? Have your actions been orienting themselves outward toward others? A caterpillar transforms into a butterfly in a matter of days. But God is patient in transforming us into the image of His Son, and He takes His time.

In 2 Corinthians 3:18, Paul uses *metamorphosis* a second time to describe the goal of our transformation—that we look like Jesus! The word *Christian* gets to this idea quite nicely; it means to be "like Jesus" in word and deed (Acts 11:26). Those first Christians in Antioch spent an entire year learning from Barnabas and Saul. You and I have the privilege for the rest of our lives of learning from God in His Word to become like His Son (1 Pet. 4:2). There is no greater journey than to come to know the truth of Jesus and *become new in Him!*

1. Review the past one hundred days in this devotional process. What has changed in your beliefs? Your thinking? Your attitudes? Your feelings toward others? Your choices? Your values? Your confidence in Christ?

2. Plan your next steps to continue "becoming new"! Perhaps your first step might be to hand this book to a friend and share how God has grown you by His Spirit through His Word.

3. Take a moment to thank God for His kind shaping in your life. The Christian life is a series of new beginnings. Sometimes we start again out of necessity, other times out of failure, and even more so out of our faith that Jesus is still calling us. Make today another new beginning.

Notes

Day 1

1. Walter Scott, *Marmion: A Tale of Flodden Field* (London: Charles Tilt, 1839), 214.

Day 7

1. Jamie Allen, "New Song List Puts 'Rainbow' Way Up High," CNN, March 7, 2001, https://edition.cnn.com/2001/SHOWBIZ/Music/03/07/365.songs/index.html.

2. Charles H. Spurgeon, "The Rainbow" (sermon, Metropolitan Tabernacle, London, June 28, 1863), www.spurgeon.org/resource-library/sermons/the-rainbow/#flipbook.

Day 9

1. Joseph Parker, "God Holds the Key" (1887), Public Domain.

Day 20

1. Ralph Waldo Emerson, "Character," in *Essays* (Philadelphia: David McKay, 1888), 108.

Day 23

1. See *Concise Oxford English Dictionary*, 11th ed. (2004), s.v. "character"; Robert L. Thomas, *New American Standard Hebrew-Aramaic and Greek Dictionaries*, rev. ed. (Anaheim: Foundation, 1998), 5480–81.

Day 24

1. Bill Watterson, *It's a Magical World* (New York: Scholastic, 1997), 146.

2. Peter Taylor Forsyth, *Positive Preaching and Modern Mind* (London: Hodder and Stoughton, 1907), 42–43.

Day 27

1. Ernest Hemingway, *Death in the Afternoon* (London: Scribner, 1932), 13.

Day 28

1. Amy Carmichael, *Kohila: The Shaping of an Indian Nurse* (London: Society for Promoting Christian Knowledge, 1939), 170.

2. Pearl S. Buck, "My Neighbor's Son," in *To My Daughters, with Love* (New York: John Day, 1967), 42.

Day 30

1. *Concise Oxford English Dictionary*, 11th ed. (2004), s.v. "hap."

2. Alexander Maclaren, quoted in Tryon Edwards, *The New Dictionary of Thoughts: A Cyclopedia of Quotations from the Best Authors of the World, Both Ancient and Modern, Alphabetically Arranged by Subjects* (Charlotte, NC: Britkin, 1927), 307.

3. Thomas Merton, *The Sign of Jonas* (San Diego: Houghton Mifflin Harcourt, 1981), 286.

Day 37

1. Benjamin Disraeli, quoted in Tryon Edwards, *The New Dictionary of Thoughts: A Cyclopedia of Quotations from the Best Authors of the World, Both Ancient and Modern, Alphabetically Arranged by Subjects* (Charlotte, NC: Britkin, 1927), 438.

2. William Arthur Ward, *Thoughts of a Christian Optimist: The Words of William Arthur Ward* (Anderson, SC: Droke, 1968), 55.

Day 38

1. Frank W. Boreham, *The Luggage of Life* (London: Charles H. Kelly, 1912), 229.

Day 42

1. Robert Law, *The Tests of Life: A Study of the First Epistle of St. John* (Edinburgh: T&T Clark, 1909), 304.

Day 43

1. D. L. Moody, quoted in Stanley and Patricia Gundry, *The Wit and Wisdom of D. L. Moody* (Chicago: Moody Press, 1974), 51.

Day 49

1. George Orwell, *Nineteen Eighty-Four* (New York: New American Library, 1952), 163.

2. Lewis Carroll, *Through the Looking-Glass, and What Alice Found There* (London: Macmillan, 1882), 124.

Interlude

1. Augustine, quoted in R. C. Sproul, "Ancient Promises," Ligonier Ministries, December 18, 2023, www.ligonier.org/learn/articles/ancient-promises#:~:text=%E2%80%9CThe%20new%20is%20in%20the,closely%20interrelated%20with%20each%20other.

Day 54

1. Augustine, quoted in Martin H. Manser, *The Westminster Collection of Christian Quotations* (Louisville, KY: Westminster John Knox, 2001), 201.

2. Charles Haddon Spurgeon, *The Salt-Cellars: Being a Collection of Proverbs, Together with Homely Notes Thereon* (New York: A. C. Armstrong and Son, 1889), 291.

Day 57

1. Robert Murray M'Cheyne, letter to Daniel Edwards, October 2, 1840, in Andrew A. Bonar, *Memoir and Remains of the Rev. Robert Murray M'Cheyne* (Dundee: William Middleton, 1846), 243.

Day 61

1. Charles Haddon Spurgeon, "Ask and Have, (sermon, Metropolitan Tabernacle, London, October 1, 1882), www.spurgeon.org/resource-library/sermons /ask-and-have/#flipbook.

Day 69

1. Mahatma Gandhi, quoted in E. Stanley Jones, *The Christ of the Indian Road* (New York: Abingdon, 1925), 126.

Day 71

1. Jonathan Edwards, *A Treatise Concerning Religious Affections, In Three Parts* (Philadelphia: James Crissy, 1821), 218.

Day 72

1. John Bradford, quoted in Fleming Rutledge, *Not Ashamed of the Gospel: Sermons from Paul's Letter to the Romans* (Grand Rapids, MI: Eerdmans, 2007), 166.

Day 75

1. Charles Haddon Spurgeon, *Gleanings among the Sheaves*, 2nd ed. (New York: Sheldon, 1869), 57.

Day 83

1. Alfred Henry Ackley, "He Lives," 1933 (copyright renewed 1961 by the Rodeheaver Co., a division of Word Music).

Day 84

1. *The Discourses of Epictetus; with the Encheiridion and Fragments*, trans. George Long (London: George Bell and Sons, 1890), 425.

Day 85

1. Martin Luther, quoted in Martin H. Manser, *The Westminster Collection of Christian Quotations* (Louisville, KY: Westminster John Knox, 2001), 21.

Day 88

1. C. T. Studd, quoted in Martin H. Manser, *The Westminster Collection of Christian Quotations* (Louisville, KY: Westminster John Knox, 2001), 329.

Day 90

1. A. W. Tozer, quoted in Peyton Jones, "In His Absence," *Christianity Today*, September 2015, www.christianitytoday.com/le/2015/september-web-exclusive /in-his-absence.html (italics mine).

Day 99

1. Lea Lane, "Is Cruising Safe? Facts and Figures to Help You Decide," *Forbes*, March 24, 2019, www.forbes.com/sites/lealane/2019/03/24/is-cruising -safe-facts-and-figures-to-help-you-decide.

2. Charles Haddon Spurgeon, *The Salt-Cellars: Being a Collection of Proverbs, Together with Homely Notes Thereon* (New York: A. C. Armstrong and Son, 1889), 188.

Scripture Index

New Testament

Meet the Editor

Many pastors around the world can tell stories about the encouragement and wisdom they received from Warren Wiersbe, but it's my distinct honor to be among the few who knew him as both spiritual guide and grandfather. My mother is the second of four children born to Warren and Betty. Of course, when she married my dad and took his name, the obvious connection to the Wiersbe family was obscured. The fact that my last name isn't Wiersbe hasn't limited my grandfather's impact on my life.

My earliest memory of Grandpa Wiersbe was that he traveled more than anyone I knew. Our family lived in the shadow of O'Hare, and our house was his frequent stop-over before his speaking engagements. We picked him up at the airport so often that, as a toddler, I dubbed the terminal "grandpa's house"! I had a better idea of his life's work in those early days, as every morning, his preaching filled our kitchen over the WMBI airwaves. I tried reading one of his books when I was ten. Of course, I was in way over my head, and I put it down after he used the word *ecclesiastical* three times in one paragraph!

When I was sixteen, I sensed a calling into pastoral ministry, and my grandpa was my chief supporter and encourager. He cheered me on while I studied at Moody Bible Institute, gifting me with so many books for my dorm room that I hardly needed the library. When I joined the pastorate and was learning to preach weekly to middle school students, Grandpa Wiersbe fed me teaching ideas and illustrations. Having a biblically proficient grandpa in my corner felt like I was cheating, but he just called it a blessing. He was my first call when I faced complex church issues, biblical questions, or challenging people. There's not an aspect of theology, devotion, church polity, pastoral ethics, preaching, or leadership that I haven't learned from him.

The relational investment my grandfather made in me is one of the precious spiritual blessings that are mine in Jesus. And I suspect if my grandfather could see the ministry continuing through our family today, he might reciprocate that feeling. In our conversations, he constantly spoke about the merits of building upon the work of prior generations. One of his books, *50 People Every Christian Should Know*, is about this very subject. He prayed for those who would come after him, that we would not just receive or reject his generation's faith but build upon it as we followed the leading of the Holy Spirit.

For the better part of two decades now, I've enjoyed serving Jesus with the same mission my grandpa had: helping others know God's heart for them as they learn to study His Word for themselves. True transformation occurs when we trust God's faithfulness to keep His promises. It's exhilarating to watch God interrupt patterns of generational ignorance as people place their faith in Jesus Christ and the old becomes new. I'm wildly optimistic that the church's future is bright as a new generation of pastors and teachers builds upon the truth of Jesus Christ, the same yesterday, today, and forever. The best is yet to come, and I thank God I get to be a part of it.

WIERSBE BIBLE STUDIES

Bible studies you can trust from world-renowned Warren W. Wiersbe

The Wiersbe Bible Study Series incorporates material from Warren's popular series of expositional commentaries (known as the "BE" series) into a small group Bible study format. These consist of a Bible book introduction, tips for small group study, self-introspective questions, and practical application. Allow your small group to delve deeper, growing in biblical understanding and practical application for today.

DAVID C COOK

transforming lives together

Trusted Commentaries
from Dr. Warren W. Wiersbe

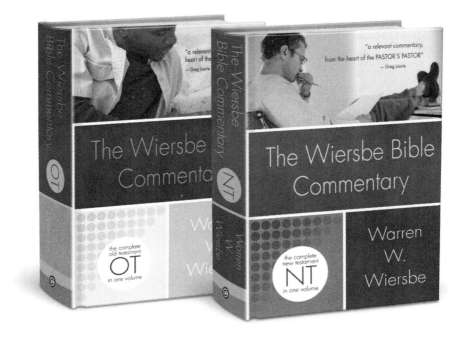

The Wiersbe Bible Commentaries offer trustworthy insights on the entire Old and New Testaments. Introductions and outlines for each book have clear, readable text that's free of academic jargon. Two volumes are available: Old Testament (Genesis through Malachi) and New Testament (Matthew though Revelation).

Whether you are a pastor, teacher, or layperson, you can study the Bible in easy-to-read sections that emphasize personal application and biblical meaning.

Available in print and digital editions
everywhere books are sold

transforming lives together